By the same author:

An Unfinished Conversation:
The Life and Music of Stan Rogers

The Luck of the Draw:
True Life Tales of Lotteries and Their Winners

Out of This World:
The Natural History of Milton Acorn

You're Not As Good As You Think You Are:
A Demotivational Guide

Consider the Fish

Fishing for Canada,
from Campbell River to Petty Harbour

Chris Gudgeon

Best fishes,
Chris G.

VIKING

VIKING

Published by the Penguin Group

Penguin Books Canada Ltd, 10 Alcorn Avenue, Toronto, Ontario, Canada M4V 3B2

Penguin Books Ltd, 27 Wrights Lane, London W8 5TZ, England

Viking Penguin, a division of Penguin Books USA Inc., 375 Hudson Street,
New York, New York 10014, U.S.A.

Penguin Books Australia Ltd, Ringwood, Victoria, Australia

Penguin Books (NZ) Ltd, cnr Rosedale and Airborne Roads, Albany, Auckland
1310, New Zealand

Penguin Books Ltd, Registered Offices: Harmondsworth, Middlesex, England

First published 1998

10 9 8 7 6 5 4 3 2 1

Stan Rogers lyrics used by permission.
All complete poems used by permission.
Illustrations of fish by permission of the Department of Fisheries and Oceans,
Canada.

Everything's true in this book, except the stuff that's made up.

Printed and bound in Canada on acid free paper ∞

CANADIAN CATALOGUING IN PUBLICATION DATA

Gudgeon, Chris, 1959–

  Consider the fish

ISBN 0-670-87164-8

1. Fisheries—Political aspects—Canada—Humor 2. Nationalism—Canada—
Humor. I. Title

SH441.G83 1998   639.2'0971   C96-930651-2

Visit Penguin Canada's web site at www.penguin.ca

In loving memory of Eric Gudgeon . . .
who knew a fish when he saw one.

I touched the flesh with my eyes.
It was that of a woman with scales.
The lips were thick and closed.
It had swallowed all my symbols.

The phantom appeared and winked.
I kept hauling it up.
The eyes were bluer than mine.
She floundered on the sand
and the sea gleamed.

I pitched my wishes back into the black water.

"Fish," by Joe Rosenblatt

Acknowledgments

Thanks to, in order of appearance: Joe Rosenblatt; Colin Munn; all the good people at Painter's Lodge, in Campbell River, British Columbia; Alan Haig-Brown; Daniel Francis; Al Purdy; Van Egan; Joe Painter; Valerie Haig-Brown; Tim Bowling; Michael Turner; *Geist* magazine; Bud Livingstone and all the good people at Kraft Foods; Jim McLennan; Neil Jennings; Mike Guinn; the Best Western Hospitality Inn in Calgary; the Orvis Company; Kerry Brewin; Frederick Wooding; Chris Hagen; everyone at the Calgary chapter of Trout Unlimited; David Arnason; the Valgardson family; Leo Kristjanson; Ted Kristjanson; Greg Long; Bill Long; David "Carp" Carpenter; Lee "Will Work for Food" Gowan; Shawn Robins; everyone at the Country Resort, where I always stay when I'm in Gimli; Ariel Rogers, and all the assorted Rogers offspring; David McFadden (whose *Great Lakes Suite* inspired this book); Scott Misner; Shawn Cafferky; Brigitte Dugal; everyone at *Canadian Wildlife* and *Sentier Chasse-Pêche*; Julian Fikus; George Grant; Mary Acorn and the entire Acorn family; Rosalee Hattie; Peter Murphy; Greg Stephenson; Cabot Martin; Patrick Lane.

Daphne Hart, my literary agent; my researcher and friend, Tony Nelson; the B.C. Arts Council; Jackie Kaiser, my editor at Penguin Books, who believed in this book before I even realized it was a book, and Meg Taylor, who took over when Jackie decided to have a baby; Wendy Thomas, the best copy editor in town; and everyone at Penguin Books Canada.

Thanks, finally, to my wife, Barb Stewart, and our three wonderful boys, Tavish, Charlie and Keating.

Contents

ᶢ

Consider the Fish . . .

Canada is a pathological lie; a fish tale which grows better with each telling . . .

—*Fillet of Soul,* Lillian Manley

L et me make one thing clear from the start: I am one of the worst anglers the Lord ever created.

I have never caught a single fish. Not one. I've had nibbles, of course. And bites. I've even had fish virtually landed, on the hook and in the net, so close to the boat that I could look deep into their little fish eyes, and see—not fear—but a deep irritation.

The closest I ever came to catching a fish was when a disorientated sockeye salmon jumped in, then out, of my rented fibreglass dinghy. That's nothing like what happened to my brother Greg. Once, he was about to give up after fishing the Oyster River for five hours when a seven-pound rainbow trout grounded itself at his feet, just in time for dinner. Then there's the fish story reported in the January 1997 issue of *Esquire* magazine, about a Brazilian fisherman named Nathon do Nascimento. At the exact moment Nathon yawned, a six-inch fish jumped out of the water and into his mouth. The poor man choked to death. These stories sound improbable, but the best fish stories—like the best love stories—

are built around the small, unlikely coincidences that lend our lives a sense of order amidst the chaos.

But my bad luck catching fish hasn't stopped me from thinking about them—even more so lately, as every day the papers are swimming with stories about Canada's troubled fisheries. Salmon wars, cod wars—it's a battlefield out there. And even though I wouldn't recognize a turbot if one bit me on the nose, I'm convinced that these fish are essential to Canada's national security.

I've noticed that the Canadian male is particularly obsessed with the pursuit and capture of fish, and I'm absolutely certain there are profound reasons for this. I have no idea what those reasons are, but I am intrigued. This obsession comes through in the work of many of our most consciously "male" artists, men like Stan Rogers and Milton Acorn, respectively Canada's greatest songwriter and Canada's greatest poet. Both were fascinating characters, who trolled the Canadian consciousness, and the depths of their own love and anger, to find inspiration for their art. Both were particularly fascinated with the fish and fishers of this country, especially Rogers, who imagined this country as one immense fishing village, and when you look at the facts, it's not such a strange idea.

Canada has the longest marine coastline in the world, fronts on three oceans, and contains 16 percent of the earth's fresh water. Meanwhile, fish generate $10 billion annually for our economy, providing millions of Canadians with livelihood and diversion. Those of us not directly involved with the fishing or sportfishing industries can't escape the impact that fish have on our economy, history and culture. But fish just don't get no respect in this country. One small case in point: while almost every province has an officially recognized bird or flower, only one—Alberta—has a provincial fish.

So I decided it was time to give the fish their due. I set off across the country on a low-budget Royal Fishin' Commission, and in the course of a year scraped up enough money to visit select fishing communities from Campbell River, British Columbia, to Petty Harbour, Newfoundland. This book is the Commission's final report; it's neither a how-to guide for budding anglers, nor a political exposé of an industry on the brink of disaster. Instead, think of it as an accidental travelogue—part popular history, part meandering, fish-eye view of a country and its people. Or better yet, as an unfolding series of fish tales, straddling fact and fiction, growing bigger and better with each telling.

By the time you finish this book, you just might have a little better understanding of the circumstances that have led up to the crisis in our fishery. Maybe not. But at the very least, you'll have a greater appreciation for fish and the impact they've had on this country. Historians and journalists focus on things like the fur trade and the railroad when they examine the soul of this country, and relegate the sole of this country to the status of economic indicator with little social significance outside of the Maritimes. This attitude betrays a central Canada bias, the same bias that has produced puzzling national icons like the beaver—chosen because it's industrious and loyal, or because it has buck teeth, interbreeds and rarely tips?—and the blood-red maple leaf. Sure, it looks good on a curler's lapel pin or a hiker's back pack, but what meaning does it hold for anyone living west of Thunder Bay?

In short, then, I'm asking you to consider the fish. Even if, like me, you've never had any luck with fish, I'm asking you to consider the fish as an important part of your daily life, your business, your personal relations. I'm asking you to forget the fur trade, the railroad, the cultural mosaic, or even the Stanley Cup, and to consider instead the fish as a key to understanding this nation's notion of what it means to be a man and as a defining image of our collective experience. I'm asking a lot, I know, but what's the point of life, if you don't take the time to smell the fish along the way?

Chapter 1

Waiting for Cabot

"As we look back on all that Cabot lived for, and what the land he found has given us, let us salute that brave sailor and pray that we may, God willing, inherit some of his marvellous vision and courage. Canada's next five hundred years will be then as glorious as its past. . . ."

—Queen Elizabeth II

Atlantic Tomcod

Beginning at the end, in Bonavista, Newfoundland

W e stood on the side of a hill in a drizzle so thick we might just as well have been underwater ourselves, a shoal of humanity staring out into the fog-clogged sea. Bonavista, Newfoundland, was the penultimate stop on my cut-rate, unofficial Royal Fishin' Commission, some three hours' drive from my final port of call, Petty Harbour. It seemed fitting to be winding down at the exact spot where fishing in Canada—the country itself—began. From where I stood, just to the left of the RCMP honour guard, I had a good view of Her Majesty Queen Elizabeth II and her husband, Prince Philip. I'd seen them before, at much closer range, but this time they seemed different. They looked, for lack of a better word, happy. I mean, they always seem happy enough at these events—all smiles and pendulum waves of the hand—but today there was a gleam in the royal eyes and you could say the Queen was actually beaming, and I can only speculate that it wasn't because of the weather. My guess is that she was brimming with pride. It wasn't just an important moment for Newfoundland, the first of a full year's worth of celebrations honouring the province's discovery and five hundredth anniversary. It was an important moment for Mother England, marking the point when, on the whim of Henry VII, she'd begun her long makeover from Europe's ugly stepsister to shining Empress of the world. The Queen, in short, was gushing in that reserved and somewhat sombre way that only a Queen can gush.

Suddenly the *Matthew* hove into sight. That's an actual word, *hove*. In fact, it's the past tense of heave, and a very nautical way of saying that suddenly, from the deep fog, a ship came into view. She was a strange sight, an almost impossibly tiny replica of John Cabot's impossibly tiny flagship. Up to that point the crowd of thirty thousand had been rather silent, perhaps listening to the strains of "I's the B'y" coming from some distant, omnipotent concertina. But all at once the crowd broke into spontaneous, unreserved applause. Even the Queen and Prince Philip joined in, though with less abandon; only the RCMP honour guard somehow managed to restrain itself. There was enough noise to almost drown out the not-too-distant drumming of a group of native protesters, led by Ovide Mercredi, former national chief of the Assembly of First Nations.

"Look, honey," I heard an America tourist beside me say to his wife. "It's Sebastian Cabot!"

"What? The actor?"

"No, honey, the explorer."

"Well, I wondered. Because I'm sure the actor is dead."

The crew of the *Matthew* stood in a neat row on the makeshift dock in Bonavista Bay. They were a happy-looking lot, perhaps pleased with the kind of attention not normally heaped on sailors in 1997, perhaps just happy to be on dry land. It had been a long, tough voyage, lasting fifty-three days—twenty days longer than the original voyage—and taking the nineteen-member crew through some pretty harsh weather, including one storm dead centre of the Atlantic that featured highway-speed winds and fifty-foot waves. Now, safe on land legs, the crew listened patiently to the Queen's welcome message, unaware that while they were braving high winds and dangerous seas, they'd been at the heart of a curiously Canadian media storm back on The Rock. It raged between the two beer giants, Molson's, who took to calling their local Black Horse brew "the unofficial beer of Cabot's crew," and Labatt's, one of the official sponsors of the modern *Matthew*'s voyage. Cheeky

7

Molson's had gone so far as to put a picture of Cabot lustfully eye-balling a beer on cases of Black Horse.

"As we look back on all that Cabot lived for," the Queen said, her former real joy now sunk by the weight of her speaking notes, "let us salute that brave sailor and pray that we may, God willing, inherit some of his marvellous vision and courage."

While it's true we'd gathered on that hill to pay homage to John Cabot, explorer, I was more interested in the undercurrent, the theme beneath the premise, the idea that had brought us all together. And what was that mysterious thing, that unifying force? Well, the answer to that question just might surprise you.

Unless, of course, you think the answer's "fish."

In that case, you probably won't be surprised at all.

The first chapter in Canadian Fhishstory begins in the spring of 1496, when King Henry VII of England granted a certain neo-phyte explorer named John Cabot a letter of patent, essentially a royal permission slip giving him exclusive rights to sail around looking for "all heathen islands or countries hitherto unknown to all Christians." Exactly where Cabot had come from remains a mystery. He might have been born Johan Cabot Montecalunyal in Genoa, Italy, in 1451, but then again, he might not. But if this was the case, he was undoubtedly playmates with another future globe-trotter, Christopher Columbus. We do know that by the early 1460s Cabot made his way to Venice, where he settled for some twenty years and learned the seafarer's trade. In those days, Venice was a major trading centre and home to some of the best mapmakers and navigators in the known world. It's here that Cabot learned the sailor's craft and, working as a merchant marine, saw the world. His travels took him deep into the heart of the Far East, where he witnessed the nuts-and-bolts problems that hampered Europeans. It was a time when Muslim middlemen were losing their grip over maritime trade routes, and Western nations, buoyed by navigational and other technical advances by the Portuguese, dreamed of a sea route to the Orient.

Early in 1443, while Cabot was working for an English engineering firm in Spain, the Christian world was rocked by the news of Christopher Columbus's discovery of what he believed was a western sea route to the Orient. There's a very good chance that Cabot met with Columbus at that time and heard first-hand the explorer's adventures and geographic theories. In any case, it seems that Cabot was overcome with an extreme case of explorer envy and decided on the spot to beat Columbus at his own game. Columbus had taken the long route to the new world, heading south along the African coast to the Canary Islands, where he caught the southeast trade winds. Cabot quite rightly believed that a north Atlantic route would be much faster.

But enough of Cabot, you're thinking. Bring on the fish. And that's where this is leading, because Cabot, despite having actually never captained a crew before or headed an expedition, began scouring Europe for a sponsor for his voyage. Labatt's not being interested at the time, he tried the old standbys, Portugal and Spain, but neither had much confidence in Cabot or his vision. So he made his way to Bristol in southwest England, a thriving fishing and port city second only to London in importance, with a merchant class known to take a risk or two if it might turn a profit. Cabot had made a good choice. Norway had just booted English fishermen off Iceland's cod banks, and the Bristol merchants were looking for other sources of income, so Cabot's plan had some built-in appeal. By coincidence, Henry VII and his entourage were making a pass through Bristol at the exact time Cabot was there. Hank heard of Cabot's plan and was intrigued.

The King had passed when Columbus came a-courting, and he wasn't about to let another Genoese explorer slip through his fingers. He immediately granted Cabot the letter of patent, giving royal approval to the plan without offering any monetary support, a strategy still used today by many Canadian publishers.

With his Dear John patent letter, Cabot was able to go to Bristol's adventure capitalists with his hand out, way out, and they reluctantly agreed to fill it. A sea route to the Orient would be nice, they said, but when you got right down to it, what they really wanted was fish, and a few unclaimed islands in the North Atlantic from which they could set up cod fishing stations and beat Norway at its own game. And there it was. Cabot had his money, although only enough to commission a small ship, not much longer than a Cabbagetown driveway, and a meagre crew of twenty men, including Cabot's three sons (Lewis, Sebastian and Santius) and, of course, a barber, so the crew could look their best if they ran into any hot babes at sea.

Cabot set sail from Bristol some time around May 1, 1497, and spent more than a month drifting westward before he spotted land. On June 24, he set ashore at a spot that may or may not have been the site of modern Bonavista—it was more likely near a place called Cape North, on Cape Breton Island, a theory championed by Canadian historians before Newfoundland joined Confederation. In any case, Cabot believed he had reached the land of the Great Khan and claimed this new land in the name of King Henry VII of England. After his landfall, Cabot cruised the coast of North America for another month, looking for riches and signs of intelligent life, which, given Cabot's chronic confusion, may have been in short supply on the *Matthew*. Eventually, with food stocks running low, Cabot headed back to England, catching favourable winds to make the trip in just over two weeks.

In London, Cabot's report of reaching the Asian shore caught more favourable wind from King Henry, who praised the discoveries and granted his pet explorer a princely pension of £20 per year. Cabot did not forget his friends in Bristol, either. He regaled them with tales of great seas of cod fish, stocks so abundant that they could be taken not "with a net, but in buckets weighed down with stones." It's likely that John Cabot wasn't even the first European of his generation to reach the New World. In all likelihood, fishermen from Bristol and from ports in Portugal and France were working the waters off North America as early as 1480, but of course, being fishermen, they kept word of their rich harvest to themselves. But Cabot wasn't one for secrets. He wanted publicity more than anything else, because publicity would bring him international fame—he could imagine Columbus turning green—and more important, publicity would bring him money to outfit a second voyage.

And the money did flow in. Overlooking the fact that Cabot hadn't returned with anything of real value like gold or spices, but excited by the prospect of an endless supply of fish, the Bristol merchants immediately ponied up for a second voyage. But this time they did it in style, outfitting six ships and three hundred men. Cabot set off again exactly one year after his initial voyage. As to the success of that trip, a contemporary historian, Polydore Vergil, wrote that Cabot was "believed to have found new lands nowhere but on the very bottom of the ocean," proving that while Cabot was probably dead in 1498, the art of sarcasm was very much alive.

11

Poor John Cabot. He not only disappeared without a trace on his second voyage, but his ungrateful middle son, Sebastian, took credit for many of his achievements, including such trivialities as the discovery of North America. Some historians believe that Sebastian even destroyed or altered documents in an effort to eclipse his lost father. And so, underappreciated for generations, the elder Cabot slowly drifted sideways into the history books, which is a fitting legacy for a man who never seemed to be completely sure of where he was going, or how he was going to get there.

In any case, he found the fish, and make no mistake about it, the fish is what brought the people to this country. No one came to Canada looking for the Orient—in fact, Canada very quickly proved to be an inconvenient impediment to anyone looking for a westward route to the Far East. And it wasn't for the furs or the lush farmland; that all would come later. Nope. We came for the fish. The earliest European residents were fishermen, who'd retreat to the rocky banks of Newfoundland, Labrador and Cape Breton to salt and dry their catch for the long voyage home. In time, some of these fishermen took native wives, or simply decided that life in this new land wasn't so bad, when you weighed everything up against everything else. And even those hardy souls whose interest lay in the fur trade would often supplement their income by catching fish.

So there it is. And as I stood on that rain-soaked hill in Bonavista, paying tribute with thirty thousand other tourists to a man of whom we know almost nothing, honouring an achievement for which there exists so few details, in a place that almost certainly wasn't the scene of his greatest triumph, I thought less about John Cabot and his marvellous vision and courage, and more about ineptitude and folly, two of humanity's greatest attributes, I think, and mostly about the forgotten fish that had brought us all together.

Chapter 2

In Cod We Trust

The history of the northeastern maritime region of North America has been dominated by the fishing industry, but it is significant that the cod, the staple fish, has secured recognition only grudgingly as the basis of economic development. Massachusetts has paid tribute to its key position; but Newfoundland and Nova Scotia have shown neglect. Whereas in Canada, the beaver was fittingly chosen as a symbol of unity, in Newfoundland the cod was largely responsible for disunity, and its lack of recognition is a result.

— *The Cod Fisheries,* Harold Innis

Atlantic Cod

A primer of Canadian Fhishstory

T he *Matthew* Landfall Ceremony was over by 3:45 p.m. and while some diehards stuck around to watch Canada Post unveil its Cabot Commemorative stamp, most of us slunk off to find something good to eat. There are a lot of nice little restaurants in Bonavista—The Baie Vista, P.K.'s Restaurant, the Harbour View Take-out, Terry's Place—but I stuck to the makeshift café at the Media Hostel. You could get a burger there for $2.50, which ain't half bad, while I myself celebrated with the Pan Fried Cod Dinner ($8.50, served with fries, dressing and vegetables). I stopped short of ordering the cod tongues, an alleged delicacy I'd sampled in St. John's a few days earlier. There's something about a pile of tiny tongues that just doesn't suit my palate. But the cod was good, and it was a fitting way—perhaps the only fitting way—to salute the return of the *Matthew*.

Considering the impact it's had on the country, there's nothing too remarkable about the cod. It's a bottom feeder—what fishermen call "groundfish"—frequently found at depths of 450 metres or more. It favours cold to downright frigid water and can be found all along Canada's eastern shore, from the Bay of Fundy to the northern tip of Labrador. The average commercially caught cod is just under two feet long and weighs four or five pounds—although that's far from the record set in 1895 off the coast of Massachusetts, when a fisherman hauled in a cod weighing 211 pounds. I shudder to think of the tongue on that thing. Cod are rather long-lived for fish. They commonly live to see their twentieth birthday, and a few have been known to reach the big three-oh. They're also energetic travellers: one cod of note was caught in the central North Sea in the summer of 1957. A scientist tagged and released the fish, and it wandered for four more years, until it was caught again off the Grand Banks, 1,900 miles away.

The most surprising thing about the cod is that it looks absolutely nothing like I thought it would. Coming from British Columbia, I'm used to rock cod and ling cod, which, although part of the same family, bear little resemblance to the Atlantic cod, the proper name for the predominant species on the east coast. Rock cod, for example, are roly-poly fish, bright orange in colour, with a set of spiky fins along the back and big, bulbous eyes; Atlantic cod have narrower, tapered bodies, which bulge in the centre, with four fins along the back, and are kind of speckled brown like a brook trout, with a telltale barb on the bottom of their lower lip. As far as fish go, they are rather homely, so it's not their good looks that account for the cod's tremendous popularity as a food fish. Even with the cod moratorium in this country, these fish are still one of the most important commercial catches in the world, and it wasn't so long ago that the single cod stock from the Grand Banks, an underwater shelf off Newfoundland's south and east coasts, fed most of Europe and parts of South America.

Canada's cod are a cash cow for four reasons. First, they taste quite okay, with a light, white, flaky meat that's not too fishy. Even people like me who don't like fish can learn to like cod. They also have a relatively uniform size and shape, which makes them easier to process and transport. Third, they're good reproducers; a single—hopefully engaged—female can produce twelve million eggs at one time. But the biggest reason for the success of the Atlantic cod is simple geography. The great cod grounds like the Labrador Banks, Georges Banks off New England and of course the Grand Banks, a 37,000-square-mile undersea plateau, larger than all Newfoundland, are at the convergence of two enormous underwater rivers, the Gulf Stream and the Labrador Current. Driven by prevailing winds and spurred on by the earth's rotation, the

Gulf Stream runs north from the Caribbean, producing a constant flow thousands of times bigger than the largest river on land and an endless source of the kind of food bottom fish fancy. The Labrador Current flows westward from Greenland, carrying with it vast numbers of voracious cod that congregate in the floating buffet at the point where the two rivers collide. The sheer volume of fish, literally billions and billions in any given season, meant that it made economic sense for fishermen to brave an ocean voyage.

Of course, cod was not the only fish the fishermen found in the New World. Salmon choked the bays and rivers along the coast during the spring and fall, lobster were so plentiful you could scoop them up in a net from shore, and there was a wide assortment of other fish waiting to be caught. Wide, but not too wide. We now know that for a country of 9,970,610 square kilometres, containing the longest coastline (some 243,790 kilometres) in the world, 16 percent of the fresh water and 9 percent of the river flow, Canada has a relatively limited selection of fish. Thanks to those bloody ice-age glaciers, which only recently—in geological terms—retreated from our soil, there are just 177 species of freshwater fish—181 if you count brown trout, carp, goldfish and tench, alien species successfully introduced to Canadian waters. Ohio, by contrast, has 170 species. As for saltwater fish, it's a little harder to get an accurate number. McAllister's authoritative 1960 *List of Marine Fishes of Canada* identifies 260 species in the Pacific region, 107 in the Arctic, and 259 in the Atlantic, for a total of 616 types of marine fish—a drop in the bucket compared to the nearly 24,000 fish species around the world.

For those who need to feel smug or inferior about this sort of thing, here is a list of the number of freshwater species per province:

Ontario	132
Quebec	105
Manitoba	79
British Columbia	71
Saskatchewan	60
Alberta	51
New Brunswick	48
Northwest Territories	41
Nova Scotia	34
Yukon Territory	31
Labrador	21
Newfoundland	20
Prince Edward Island	19

What Canada lacks in quantity it makes up for in quality. Freshwater species such as various trout, salmon, whitefish and pike are prized by anglers and commercial fishers alike, while half a dozen marine species have, until recently, been the backbone of significant regional industries: groundfish, particularly the cod, and lobster in the Atlantic; salmon and groundfish, particularly halibut and hake, in the Pacific; and herring on both coasts. Even in this age of decline, the commercial catch is worth about $1.5 billion each year—which is roughly equal to the amount the federal government spent on its retraining programs for unemployed Atlantic fishermen—while processing generates another $3 billion. The total value of the commercial, commercial sport, sport and native food fisheries in the country is probably in the neighbourhood of

$10 billion. That sounds like a lot, but when you consider that it amounted to less than 2 percent of Canada's Gross Domestic Product, you can understand why we often overlook the humble fish. And while Canada is usually among the top twenty countries when it comes to catch volumes, we lag well behind the big four producers: Japan, Russia, China and the United States; instead, we're in a league with nations like South Korea, Iceland, Mexico and Spain. In all, Canada's share of the world catch hovers around 2 percent of the total, and what we do catch, we process; 95 percent of the catch is used for food—with the bulk of that filleted and sold "fresh," that is, chilled on ice or frozen. The remaining 5 percent is used for fertilizer or food for pets and livestock. We also favour the export market; each year, Canada ships out 80 percent of its catch, with half going to the United States, and a fifth headed to Japan. At the same time, we import half a billion dollars' worth of seafood; the seaweed, it seems, is always greener on the other side of the ocean.

Meanwhile, sportfishing is one of Canada's most popular pastimes, enjoyed by almost one-fifth of the population, and another million or more visitors each year. In 1990—the last year for which there are accurate figures—anglers caught 300 million fish in Canadian waters, and 157 million of those were keepers. That's a lot of fish, and a lot of fish stories.

Isn't it amazing how much of the history of the Western world has been driven by the endless search for a tasty meal? Take the spice trade, for example. Back in the old days before refrigerators or microwaves or monocalcium phosphate, food spoiled quickly, particularly meat, that valuable protein source, and particularly meat in Mediterranean countries, where it wasn't just the humidity, it was the heat that did meat in. Diners needed spices to make their meals palatable, and that simple craving sparked what would be, in today's terms, a multi-billion-dollar industry. The spice trade was the biggest thing going, creating fortunes and entire city-states, and providing Europe's power brokers with the incentive to mount a string of crusades against those infidels who just happened to control the Middle Eastern trade routes.

The exact same forces were behind the rush to the new-found fisheries off the new-found lands. Within a few years of the *Matthew*'s voyage, English, Breton, Norman, Spanish, Basque and Portuguese fishermen were regularly trolling the waters on the far side of the Atlantic, and there's a lot of evidence to suggest that the last group established a settlement near Ingonish on Cape Breton Island as early as 1520. In his journals, the French explorer Samuel de Champlain mentions that Basque fishermen were already fishing from Prince Edward Island in 1623 and had probably done so for years. There's some evidence that these Basques came ashore to dry their catch and may have even established temporary settlements on the Island. By 1585, there were more than three hundred vessels and six thousand men fishing off Canada's Atlantic coast. The Brits were particularly aggressive, setting up shop in Newfoundland near the richest cod-breeding grounds. The vast majority of the cod they caught was destined for the Mediterranean, providing a product that would quickly become a Friday supper staple, thanks to the Church's once-a-week meat ban.

By the start of the seventeenth century, France and England were the main rivals in the Canadian Atlantic fishery. The French concentrated on the St. Lawrence and the deepwater banks off Labrador, while the English had firmly established Newfoundland as their fishing base. At first, the fishery had been seasonal, with fishermen arriving in the spring, working through the summer, and returning to their home port by early fall. On land, they'd set up temporary shelter beneath a sail roof, in little curing huts made with branches from the stunted fir trees that dotted the shore. Some cod were simply cleaned, split and packed in salt, but most of it was lightly salted then left to dry in the sun on vented tables called "flakes." This method was favoured by British fishermen and resulted in a product with a much longer shelf life; in fact, because of its popularity as a ready-to-eat lunch or dinner item, hard-cured cod was the world's first fast food.

It wasn't long before some of the fishermen took native wives and opted to stay in the New World all year round. There were even some attempts to establish permanent fishing colonies. A Frenchman named Nicolas Denys was the first to try it. He started out with a handful of boats in 1633, with a home port at what's today called Liverpool, in southwestern Nova Scotia. He did so well that he returned the following year with two hundred boats. But at the end of that season, the Portuguese port authority stripped him of his ships and profits during a layover in Lisbon. He made a few other attempts, but ultimately gave up in the face of steady British conquest of the region. Denys is also notable for being one of the first to recognize the problems caused by overfishing in the New World. In his *Description of the Natural History of Acadia*, published in 1672, he complained that there were few empty harbours on Prince Edward Island, and the fishery was suffering the effects of overfishing. "This thins out the cod immensely, and makes them depart," Denys wrote. "And the quality of cod taken makes the mackerel leave also, and the herring which the cod chases. The result is that fishermen are no longer finding fish in the usual grounds."

A few enterprising Englishmen also made some attempts to set up permanent fishing bases in Newfoundland—which Britain had claimed for its own—but pragmatic forces worked against them. For starters, life on The Rock was harsh, and there was very little usable farmland. More important, those powerful

Bristol merchants, who'd bankrolled Cabot in the first place, did not want anyone setting up shop in the New World. As it stood, virtually all of the fish caught by British fishermen were sent directly to Bristol, before being dispersed throughout Christendom. This tiny bit of greed may seem inconsequential, but it had ramifications that can be felt today. First, New England, which was not under the thumb of the Bristol merchants and could trade directly with Europe and South America, emerged as the vital commercial centre in the New World. Second, Newfoundland itself developed without a strong mercantile base; it was less a colony than a perpetual fish-production machine. The result was that Newfoundland's economy lacked an overriding entrepreneurial spirit, but gained an over-reliance on fish. And as we've come to know, those fish are slippery customers.

It's hard to overstate the importance of cod to England at that time. Without a foothold in South America, where the real money was, or a feel for the fur trade, which was still very much a French thing, England had very little left to offer the world as trade bait. But they did have cod. And lots of it. Thanks to the cod, England grew as an economic power and wisely invested a lot of its money in fish futures. In other words, it built up its navy and merchant marine, in part to expand its financial base, but mostly to secure the investments it already had.

By 1700, the lay of the New World was pretty much established. Britain was entrenched in the fish-based economies of New England and Newfoundland, with some other Atlantic enclaves, while France had a grip on the fur trade and a strong colonial base in New France. Their most important fishing centres at that time were probably on Cape Breton Island, or Isle Royale as it was known at the time, and Isle St. Jean, Prince Edward Island. A 1728 census showed that, of the 422 white people living on St. Jean at the time, 125 were fishermen. The English had made some forays in the fur trade through Hudson Bay, but it was nothing to write home about.

In many ways, the relationship of the two countries in the New World mirrored their relationship in the old. They were uncomfortable neighbours, each emerging world powers, each a threat to the other's economic and personal security. As hostilities boiled over into full-fledged war at home, the colonies followed suit. The feature-length War of the League of Augsburg began in 1689 and, after seven years of fighting, settled nothing. So the superpowers went at it again in a double bill we've come to call the War of Spanish Succession. It lasted from 1702 to 1713 and ended with the Treaty of Utrecht and some major-league losses by the French. They were kicked out of Hudson Bay, Nova Scotia and Newfoundland, although French fishermen were still allowed to dry their catch along the French Shore, Newfoundland's north coast.

While Britain emerged as the winner, the war years had taken a toll on His Majesty's fishery. In 1690, the government had banned fishing boats from crossing the Atlantic; the King wanted every available ship for the navy. The fishery was left to Newfoundland's few thousand permanent residents, who were continually harassed by the French. By the time of the signing of the Treaty of Utrecht in 1713, the fishery had collapsed; in 1715, England managed to send only one fishing boat to the Grand Banks.

Meanwhile, the defeated French were left with only Prince Edward Island and Cape Breton, where they built the remarkable walled city of Louisbourg, the biggest fortress in North America. But Louisbourg wasn't just a military base. It was a fortified home to France's trade interests, particularly its fishery, on the Atlantic coast.

Relations between France and England were distant but fairly cordial over the next thirty years, with the odd invasion and attack thrown in to keep everyone on their toes. But by the 1750s, things were at an all-time low. In 1755, Governor Charles Lawrence of Nova Scotia had ordered the Acadians out, and a year later, Britain and France were at war again, prompted by France's attempts to keep its rival out of the Ohio valley. Within two years, Louisbourg had fallen, and soon Quebec City and Montreal would fly the British flag. The Peace of Paris marked the end of the Seven Years' War and formalized what everyone had known since 1760: France was finished as a force in North America. The treaty, signed in 1763, called for France to give up everything except for St. Pierre and Miquelon, tiny fishing islands off the southern coast of Newfoundland, and limited French fishermen to the waters off the big island's northern and western shores.

As England solidified its hold on Newfoundland, the fishing industry grew. By 1750, sixteen thousand men were working in the Atlantic fishery, and the total catch exceeded fifty-five million pounds. Twenty years later, there were twenty thousand men in the industry, and the catch exceeded eighty-three million pounds. Even the American Revolution barely slowed production. Although many fishermen were shanghaied by the Royal Navy, and trade routes were disrupted, the British managed to keep the cod flowing, and by the end of the Revolution, with the American and French fishing fleets devastated by the war, the Brits were poised to prosper. Typically, fish were on the table when British and American negotiators sat to hammer out the post-Revolution treaty. The Americans wanted free access to cod along the Atlantic shore, but Britain, led by Nova Scotia and Newfoundland, wanted to keep the interlopers out. In the end a compromise was reached;

the Americans could continue to fish the Gulf of St. Lawrence, but they could land to cure their fish only on unsettled shores.

The compromise didn't play well in Halifax. Before the Revolution, there was some question as to where the sympathies of Halifax's townspeople lay. After all, three-quarters of the population was Yankee, with roots in New England. But the city was a trade centre, tied to the market of London, and, in the absence of any serious naval threat from the Americans, Haligonians cast in their lot with Britain. Given the final negotiated settlement, many must have wondered if they'd made the right choice. They understood that the rules were in place as much to stem the huge black market between their city and New England as to protect Britain's fishing interests. London wanted to ensure its position as a trade centre; all products from the colonies had to run through London first.

And on and on it went, with the cod fishery growing and fish at the heart of much of the diplomacy between the newly united states and the slowly emerging nation of Canada. By the 1780s, record catches were the norm, peaking in 1788 when British fishermen took 112 million pounds of cod. But the market was flooded, fish prices crashed, and fishermen and merchants alike went bankrupt.

But you can't keep a good fish down. Within three years the market was recovering, and by the turn of the century the cod fishery was back in full swing and Canada—with fishing leading the charge—was well on its way to becoming a country.

It was a transitional time for the British Empire. In the face of lessons it learned in the American Revolution—and in light of the ongoing civil disorder in France—England allowed its colonies greater freedom. By the dawn of the nineteenth century,

Newfoundlanders were still under a naval governorship, but England allowed them to trade directly with Spain, Portugal and the British West Indies, supplier of those Canadian frontier staples, sugar and rum.

By 1815, the fishing fleet was almost completely owned by locals, and the salt fish trade was the exclusive property of Newfoundlanders. The Maritime colonies were thriving as well. The influx of Loyalists, along with Scottish and Irish immigrants, helped the population explode, from fifteen thousand to seventy-five thousand, in less than twelve years. Preferential British tariffs, like the Corn Laws, and yet another war between France and England boosted the position particularly of Nova Scotia, but of New Brunswick and Prince Edward Island as well. The Maritime colonies began to diversify their economies, concentrating on the fishery-related industries of timber and shipbuilding.

The War of 1812 further strengthened the position of Canada's domestic fisheries. In the convention that followed the war, negotiators established a three-mile limit, a kind of nautical border that gave each country control of the waters off its shores. Foreign fishermen could sail within this limit only to seek a safe harbour during a storm or to take on supplies. It was an arrangement that favoured the British colonists much more than the Americans, since the best fishing was in the waters north of the Bay of Fundy.

The colonies found it impossible to police the new fishing regulations, and appealed to London to step in and do something about rampant violations by American fishermen. The people of Prince Edward Island were particularly upset. Yankee fishing fleets favoured the cod waters around the Island, sending six hundred of its two thousand schooners to the area. But Britain was seeking to smooth out its relationship with the United States, which was looking more and more like an attractive trading partner, and was reluctant to pressure the Americans. At the same time, things were changing in the fishing industry. Boats were getting bigger and more expensive, and with technological advances like the purse seine—a type of net developed by American fishermen that closes at the top by means of a heavy drawstring—and long lines, the fish business was becoming more competitive. Smaller, independent operators couldn't compete. In desperation, Nova Scotia urged the British colonies to form a united front against American fishing interests, but Newfoundland, always wary of mainlanders, rejected the idea. The last straw for Nova Scotia and Prince Edward Island came in 1854 with yet another negotiated settlement, the Reciprocity Treaty, which granted all fishermen equal access to waters north of the 39th Parallel in return for allowing Canadian fishermen duty-free access to the American market. The Maritime colonies realized that they could not compete with the powerful U.S. merchants.

The outbreak of the American Civil War in 1861, and London's insistence that the colonies take greater responsibility for their own defence, worked to increase the sense of uncertainty throughout British North America. Finally, in 1865, the Americans cancelled the Reciprocity Treaty. They'd still presume free access to Canadian fishing grounds, but would no longer grant Canadian fish free access to their markets. And so on July 1, 1867, desperate for a larger market for its fish and timber, Nova Scotia and New Brunswick joined Ontario and Quebec to form the Dominion of Canada. Newfoundland, secure in its isolation, abstained, while Prince Edward Island wavered. Of all the British colonies, Prince Edward Island's fishery had been built up by an influx of American capital. And while the end of reciprocity came with some tough economic penalties—including a two-dollar-a-barrel tariff for fish entering the United States—many, if not most, Islanders felt that their future would be much more secure in the American fold. Prince Edward Island began serious negotiations with the

United States, and offered to waive the three-mile limit in exchange for a free trade agreement. In 1871, though, Britain, the United States and Canada, sitting at the negotiating table for the first time as an independent nation, signed the Treaty of Washington, which restored free trade; Prince Edward Island had lost its bargaining chip. Lured by Ottawa's promise of cash payments to buy out absentee landowners, and to cover the cost of the railroad, which had almost bankrupted the island, Prince Edward Island began to seriously consider Confederation. A final promise to create a ferry system linking Prince Edward Island's fish market to the rest of Canada sealed the deal. The Island joined Canada in 1873.

Fish were at the very heart of the new Dominion of Canada—which, by the way, Sir John A. Macdonald originally wanted to name the Kingdom of Canada. He wanted to emphasize our independence from Britain, but London would have none of that. It was up to Leonard Tilley, the Liberal leader of New Brunswick's government, to suggest the alternative, which he'd come across while thumbing through his family bible. Psalm 72, verse 8, to be exact: "He shall have dominion from sea to sea, and from the river unto the world's end." The verse also gave us our national motto, "from sea to sea," which was a nifty bit of foresight, since British Columbia and its sea didn't join Confederation until 1871. Now, of course, the motto appears a little shortsighted to some, as a group of concerned citizens from the north is urging the Canadian government to recognize the geographic realities of this country, and change our national slogan to "from sea to sea to sea."

But I've got a better suggestion. How about: "Three cheers for the fish!"

From Confederation on, the fishery in this country became more and more fragmented and regional, so it's hard to talk of a single Canadian fishery history after 1867. But there were some developments that had national ramifications. The biggest changes came with the creation of the Dominion government. The British North America Act, the legislation that created Canada in 1867, gave the federal government control over both saltwater and freshwater fisheries. Within a few years, however, many of the provinces realized they'd made a horrible mistake by handing the feds power over this moneymaking resource. They went to court to try to reclaim ownership of their waters, but were unsuccessful. Today, virtually all saltwater and anadromous fish—which, like salmon, spend time in both salt and fresh water—are under the thumb of the feds. And while Ottawa still makes the rules for freshwater fish, provinces usually oversee licensing and regulate environmental standards. This division of powers underlies an odd attitude Canadians have towards fish. In every province except New Brunswick and Quebec—where the rules permit private ownership of fishing rights—fish are regarded as common property. People do not buy the rights to use this resource, like they would a tree or a gold mine. They simply acquire the right by catching the fish. Finders keepers. As democratic as it may sound, this attitude has encouraged people to catch as many fish as they possibly can, and in the long term has contributed to the nationwide collapse of the fishery.

But few were worried about fish stocks at the time of Confederation. The fisheries on both coasts, and in the Great Lakes, were doing well. In 1873, Britain and the United States, with Canada at the table as an official observer, signed the Treaty of

Washington, which restored the rather uncomfortable arrangement that had existed under reciprocity. However, for the first time American fishermen openly admitted that Canada's fishery was much more valuable, and in 1888, in a deal brokered by the International Court at The Hague, the Americans agreed to what came to be called "The Halifax Award." This was a $5.5-million cash payment—$1 million to Newfoundland, and an astronomical $4.5 million to Canada—for use of harbours and access to fishing grounds. With rare foresight, Ottawa put the money away and used the interest to subsidize the upgrading of the fishing fleet.

It was the heyday of the Atlantic fishery. Nova Scotia and Newfoundland each boasted thirty thousand fishermen. But as the decade of the 1880s came to a close, the salt cod trade was slowly declining. Many of the older ports on the Atlantic were growing obsolete, unable to handle the newer, bigger fish boats. As well, beet sugar was replacing cane sugar, and the economy of the West Indies, always a strong market for salt cod, was entering a recession. The development of the New World, particularly railways, and the relative peace of the old, meant that other food sources were becoming more readily available to consumers around the world. But the final development hurt the most. People, particularly in the ever-expanding American market, no longer wanted salt cod; they wanted fresh fish, shipped by rail from Boston, or delivered each day by the fish boats of the Great Lakes.

By the turn of the century, technological advances were revolutionizing the fishing industry. Gas-powered boats had appeared on the scene. They were smaller, and less expensive to own and maintain than the old sailboat and steamers. These new boats opened up the business of fishing a little, taking the wind out of the sails of the few powerful—and often American-owned—companies that dominated the industry.

Meanwhile, the salmon canning business was having an enormous impact on Canada's west coast fishery. British Columbia had joined the Dominion in 1871, spurred by fears of American conquest and Ottawa's promise of a railway line to connect the most western British colonies with markets in central Canada and, ultimately, Mother England. Coincidentally, as Canadian Pacific Railroad honcho Donald Smith hammered the last spike at Craigellachie, a new technology was being introduced to British Columbia fisheries, a technology that would revolutionize the way people around the world thought about fish, fishing and this country. Canneries first appeared on the Skeena River, on British Columbia's north coast, in 1875, but consumers didn't take to canned salmon until railroads opened up the marketplace. Like the railroad, the canned salmon industry was a perfect symbol of Canada's entry into the machine age, speaking to the industrial age just as microwave toast and Big Macs speak to this age of instant information. It must have seemed that God had made salmon just to be canned; they arrived at the cannery doors in one great mass during the spring and fall spawning seasons, practically jumping into the can. No need to salt or dry the fish, they could be processed within hours of death. Freshly dead, cooked in a tin can, transported directly to England to be labelled and sent on their way again; by these fish did the world come to know this country.

By the turn of the century, British Columbia's salmon industry was the top fishery in the country, out-earning the cod, herring and lobster fisheries combined. Up and down the coast, there were a hundred canneries—thirty at the mouth of the Fraser alone—employing thousands of workers, most of them native, many of them Chinese. Sockeye, by virtue of its high oil content and its rust-red meat, was the most popular product. But pink, steelhead, coho, even chum—all migrated to the great canneries along the Fraser and Skeena rivers. By now, the business was almost fully mechanized thanks to the Iron Chink, a fish-rendering machine with a name that perfectly reflected the deep racial divisions that have scarred British Columbia's fishing history to this day. The Iron Chink helped propel British Columbia's salmon industry to the forefront in the country; by 1917, the province's fishery was outproducing the Maritimes'. That year, B.C.'s canneries shipped 8,567,409 forty-eight-pound cases of salmon. That equalled 411,235,632 pounds of salmon, or approximately fifty-nine pounds of salmon for every man, woman and child in the Dominion— although the men, women and children of this Dominion rarely ate Canadian canned salmon. It was too good, too valuable. Instead, we bought cheaper Alaskan salmon and fed the world with our own.

Canneries were having an impact on the east coast as well, particularly on Prince Edward Island, where lobster patiently waited for commercial exploitation. The problem with these shellfish was that they had to be cooked while they were still alive, or else the meat would spoil, and they weren't suited to other kinds of processing like salting or drying. By the 1870s, the canning industry hit Prince Edward Island, and lobsters were an immediate hit. In 1873, there were two canneries in Charlottetown, which shipped 6,711 pounds of lobster. Ten years later, Prince Edward Island was shipping out five million pounds of lobster a year, and the industry was bringing in $2 million to the local economy. Soon, other Maritime provinces caught lobster fever, and by the start of the new century these shellfish were second only to cod as the single most valuable fishery on much of the east coast.

But technology can move only so fast in this land of caution, and as the processing sector pressed ahead, actual fishing techniques and equipment lagged behind those of other maritime nations. The biggest issue was otter trawlers, large steam-driven fish boats that dragged nets behind them. Now, net fishing from boats wasn't new, but these new boats could haul bigger, heavier nets, at much greater depths than ever before. The fishermen of the day were still catching cod on hand-held lines: they quite rightly saw the trawlers, and the smaller draggers, as a threat to their traditional way of life. The independent fishermen complained that they could not compete with these expensive fishing machines. The government sided with the fishermen and put heavy restrictions on Canadian trawlers, banning them from fishing within the three-mile limit, then, in 1915, creating a special twelve-mile limit for Canadian trawlers only. The situation was absurd. Foreign trawlers had more access to our fishery than Canadian ones. But that's why I love Canada, where a rule's a rule, no matter how stupid it is.

In 1931, Ottawa introduced new rules that imposed a prohibitive $500 licence fee on trawlers, required applicants to prove that their trawler would be more productive than a traditional hand-line operation, and decreed that all new trawlers must be built in Canada. The new rules served their darker purpose; within five years, Canada's meagre trawler fleet was cut in half, from six boats to three. Meanwhile, the world's fisheries modernized: the United States had some 115 trawlers, and hundreds of other smaller power boats, while the United Kingdom had some 1,230 trawlers. But Canada seemed content to let its fishery falter; while the government was busy restricting trawlers, it was doing precious little to develop the industry.

The government began to ease its restrictions on draggers and trawlers after the Second World War, but by then, the damage had been done. Politicians wanted to maintain the highest possible employment levels in the industry—it's true, the old ways were more labour intensive—but the net result was that productivity dropped far below that of other fishing nations, and in the process, individual fishermen watched their income flounder and sink. A once thriving industry was dissolving. Neither Ottawa nor its provincial counterparts were doing much to stimulate growth in the fishery, and there was little incentive for investors, no special schools to help foster such maritime arts as seamanship, marine architecture, navigation or fishery sciences, no shipbuilding, virtually no merchant marine. Canada had become a maritime nation without a maritime soul.

✓

The fish, she is a cruel mistress, *la belle pêche sans merci*. She can make a country, or she can bring a country to its knees. Newfoundland is a case in point. In 1867, the people of The Rock decided not to join the Canadian Confederation, believing that they were strong enough to make it on their own. In the years directly following, it seemed like Newfoundlanders had made the right choice. Newfoundland fared well, bolstered by bumper fish crops, and the government attempted to diversify the economy. In 1881, workers broke ground for the Newfoundland Railway, and outport fishermen were offered healthy incentives to try their hand at farming. But a series of heartbreaks stopped the island's development cold. In 1892, a fire destroyed much of St. John's, and the country was stuck with the bill for rebuilding the city. The following year saw the worst cod catch in living memory, and soon afterwards, Newfoundland's banks collapsed. The island was feeling the effects of the world's first Great Depression.

In the face of these disasters, Newfoundland looked to the cod fishery for relief. But two problems that harked back to the 1700s were limiting any chance Newfoundland had of recovery. First, there was the question of the French Shore; the Treaty of Utrecht in 1713 had granted France exclusive fishing rights to the western shore of Newfoundland, and the island was stuck with a foreign power controlling a huge chunk of its soil. The second issue was the limited access to Newfoundland's waters granted to the Americans by the 1783 Treaty of Versailles. Newfoundland appealed to Britain for help, and in 1904 London solved the first problem by trading a nice bit of real estate in West Africa to France in exchange for Newfoundland's western shore. The following year, St. John's restricted American access to capelin and other bait fish. The Yanks took the matter to the International Court at The Hague, which eventually ruled in Newfoundland's favour. Not only did the court uphold the baitfish restrictions, it withdrew the U.S. right to fish in Newfoundland's waters.

Still, history was not on Newfoundland's side. In order to survive in the world market, Newfoundlanders had learned to be extremely competitive merchants. This served them well enough to the 1880s, when they had a lock on a sizable salt fish trade. But with advances in fishing and processing technologies, the world suddenly got a lot smaller. As we've already seen, a dozen new countries had entered the fish business by the early 1900s, and that cut into Newfoundland's trade. The First World War brought some relief to The Rock, and Newfoundlanders gave their all to the war effort. But in the aftermath of the Allied victory, they found themselves $20 million in debt. As the world slipped into another Great Depression, inflation caused that debt to skyrocket.

Meanwhile, old habits, like the cod, were dying hard. The every-man-for-himself attitude that had served the Newfoundland fishery in the boom years was now undermining the industry and taking the country down with it. There was little co-operation on the island; in St. John's, there was a large concentration of cod merchants, dealing directly with overseas markets, who saw themselves in direct competition with the individual outports. And stress the word "individual," because in the outports it was every businessman for himself. With so much internal wrangling going on, and so many people fighting for the same dollar, merchants and outport agents constantly undercut one another, and the fishermen came out the losers. In a bad year of fishing, they could expect a low return on their catch, and would barely be able to cover their costs. In a good year, things could even be worse, because a glut of cod could drive the prices way down.

In 1912, the colonial government tried to get things under control by forcing exporters to get a licence from the fishery's ministry before they could do business. But the Supreme Court shot down this new regulation. St. John's tried again the following year, this time issuing the directive under the mandate of the War Measures Act, that catch-all piece of legislation that lets a government do whatever it pleases in the face of "real or apprehended" crisis. By the 1920s, new legislation required that merchants have a special licence to export salt cod, but the rules did little good. In the face of a collapsing market, desperate exporters sold their fish wherever they could for whatever price they could get. Newfoundland's salt fish industry was in utter disarray, and by the end of the decade, the fishery had fallen behind pulp and paper in economic importance, and was quickly losing ground to mining.

But infighting wasn't the only problem with the fishery. Owners and fishermen were reluctant to modernize and adapt to changing conditions. Technological innovations like longlines and trawlers were resisted and blocked at every turn; the fishermen feared—and rightly so—that such changes threatened their traditional way of life. But they were just so damned more efficient, and allowed the American and European fishing fleets to work at a much higher profit margin. No longer able to compete on the world market, the outdated Newfoundland fishery competed with itself. On top of everything else, Newfoundland's population had reached 220,000, and the island could not support all these people on its own. Newfoundlanders depended on Britain, the United States, Canada and, to a lesser extent, the Caribbean for virtually everything other than wood and fish. That meant that consumer goods were expensive, which in turn reduced the profit margin on the fishery. In the 1929–30 season, fishermen caught sixty-nine thousand tons of fish, with a landed value of $11.5 million; the very next season, they caught six thousand tons less, but the landed value was a mere $7.7 million. The country faced bankruptcy, and the government once again appealed to Britain for help. London commissioned a Royal Commission to study the postwar salt cod industry, headed by one Lord Amulree. His Lordship's final recommendations included an absolute condemnation of the cod fisheries.

All that the fishing industry could show as a result of years of unrestricted individualism was (1) the loss of first place in the markets for heavy-salted fish and the virtual impoverishment of the Labrador fishery, (2) a severe decline in the Bank fishery, (3) a deterioration in the cure in the shore fishery, as well as the Bank and Labrador fisheries, (4) the pauperisation of large sections of the population owing partly to the operation of the credit system and partly to a series of years of low prices, (5) an all-around depletion of vessels and gear and a deterioration of equipment, (6) an entire absence of organization or cooperative effort, (7) the continuance of internal jealousies among exporters, carried to lengths which had the effect of depressing prices in foreign markets and this in the long run depriving the fisherman of the full reward for his labour, and (8) the absence of suitable local shipping for carrying fish to market, giving rise to the now almost universal practice of chartering Scandinavian vessels for the purpose.

The report wasn't just an attack on an industry, it was a manifesto that struck at the political heart of the fishery culture. In those dark days, nearly every politician was in the pocket of one fishery organization or another, and public policy decisions were never made in the public interest. What I'm trying to say, in the nicest way possible, is that the system was corrupt and self-serving, and stunk to its very core. Lord Amulree concurred: he berated the "fishocracy" of the St. John's merchants for "conducting their business on a basis of pure individualism without regard for the true interests of the country," and called for the end of responsible government as the only way out of the economic mess. In other words, throw the corrupt bastards out. The British government accepted Amulree's suggestion, and in 1934, thanks to some saucy little codfish, Newfoundland's democratic system was suspended, and the leadership of the province was handed over to an appointed board headed by a governor hand-picked in London. *La belle pêche sans merci.*

The last item on our Canadian Fhishstory menu is frozen fish sticks. And, as difficult as this may be to swallow, this diced and iced product was the unsavoury saviour of Canada's fishing industry. We can credit New Englanders for getting the frozen fish ball rolling. They came up with two innovations: a method of quick freezing that left a fish that was much better than the mushy, bland, slow-frozen fish available at the time; and filleting at point of production, which added much-needed shelf life to the

extremely perishable dead fish, while lowering weights and therefore transportation costs. The leftover fish bits, called offal, could
also be processed for fertilizer, vitamins and industrial oils. Soon,
some genius put these two innovations together and got frozen
fish fillets, the backbone of a backbone-removed industry that
flourished after the Second World War.

The beauty of frozen fish fillets is that they're a relatively stan-
dardized product, which companies could easily package and market under brand names. And they're a quick eat. Just throw them
in the oven and they're ready in a matter of minutes. The demand
for fresh fillets and frozen fillets was huge, with the central United
States hands down the biggest consumer.

The rise of this industry could not have come at a better time.
With the salt fish trade collapsing, fishermen across the country
were looking for new markets. And, as hard as this may be to
believe, Canada's transportation industry was actually ready,
willing and able to support them. The first refrigerator express
rail car had rolled out of Truro, Nova Scotia, in 1913, with a load
of fresh fish for Montreal. By 1917, the "Sea Food Special" was
making weekly runs from Mulgrave, Nova Scotia, to Halifax to
Toronto and points in between, and cold Maritime fish was haute
cuisine in the urban centres of the nation. Even the federal government got into the act, subsidizing refrigerated railcars from
both coasts. By the end of the Second World War, Canada was
supplying the United States with 90 percent of its frozen groundfish fillets.

Meanwhile, in Newfoundland, fresh and frozen fish continued
to influence the political climate of the land. That island country
had been struggling since the Great Depression. In most of Canada
one in every five adult men was out of work, while in parts of the
Maritimes, that figure rose to well above 50 percent. However, even
Canada's conservative fishery had adapted faster than that of

Newfoundland. Nova Scotia and the Great Lakes led the way into the huge American fresh and frozen fish markets, and adapted as best they could to the changing tastes of the fish-eating public. But Newfoundland dragged its heels. The island lacked a ready market for fresh fish and didn't have the capital to expand into the frozen fish industry. And at the heart of everything was the traditional outport way of life, which revolved around a lower-volume handline and dory fishery. The frozen fish industry needed lots of product and a greater concentration of resources.

The Second World War brought relief to Newfoundland's fishery. With Europe in turmoil, the island's cod was once again in demand, and the very nature of the war—with its reliance on aircraft, and the extensive presence of submarines in the Atlantic—meant that Newfoundland's position between North America and Europe was of strategic importance. Newfoundland became a first and last stop for ships or aircraft crossing the ocean. The increased activity provided Newfoundland with the capital it needed to modernize its processing plants and move into the fast frozen fillet; by the end of the war, there were forty-four brand-spanking-new filleting and freezing plants, and cod prices had climbed to three times their pre-war levels. The prosperity continued after the war, riding the growth in the mining, pulp and paper, and fishing industries, and while Newfoundland faced the future with newfound confidence, many who'd lived through the First World War didn't believe that this new prosperity would last.

In 1946, the British government decided that Newfoundland was ready to choose its own path. It called for a national referendum on Newfoundland's future, and in July of 1948, Newfoundlanders went to the polls to decide their fate: would they restore responsible government on a national basis, or would they choose, once and for all, to cast in their lot with Confederation? It was a tough choice. On the pro-Confederation side were Joey Smallwood and the people of Newfoundland's outport communities—the fishermen and their families—who believed that the Canadian government would market their fish, supply the capital needed to further modernize, and provide the common people with social services and better education. On the other hand, the St. John's merchants opposed Confederation, fearing that the loss of protective tariffs would lead to a Canadian takeover of fishing, mining and forestry. The merchants believed that The Rock could secure its future by allowing the U.S. army to set up bases on the island. In exchange, the theory went, the Americans would allow Newfoundland free access to its markets. It was a close call, with the pro-Confederation side winning only 52 percent of the votes; the fishermen had beaten the fishmongers, and Confederation was complete.

And the fish sticks just kept on coming. . . . Made from frozen blocks of fillets and fish waste, which were sawed, then battered and baked before being refrozen, they became the hottest entry in the frozen foods sweepstakes. From the dawn of the fish stick in 1952 to the death of President Kennedy, U.S. fish consumption increased 250 percent. In the tiny town of Glouster, Nova Scotia, there were six fish stick factories, prompting the *Fishing Gazette Annual Review* of 1958 to crow that seven hundred people were being employed by these factories, and even the "women earned as much as $3.60 per hour, unheard of in Glouster-town."

The 1950s and 1960s were boom years for Canada's fisheries. They'd grown, thanks to processing and packaging innovations, an expanding market and unprecedented support from the federal government, which introduced measures to stimulate fleet and processing upgrades and provide fishermen with affordable insurance.

From the end of the war to the mid-1960s, fish prices increased at a rate twice the average for other consumer products. At first, prices rose on luxury fish like salmon and lobster, but as freezing techniques improved, the value of groundfish like cod and halibut also increased.

As usual, the west coast led the way. British Columbia fishermen were quick to modernize, switching to bigger, more powerful boats that required smaller crews, and consolidating the fishery in a few large centres along the coast, but even Maritimers gave up their dories for draggers and seiners. By 1965, there were eighty-five thousand fishermen in Canada, although a third of these were only part-timers. Investment in the industry was high—some half a billion dollars in equipment and manufacturing facilities—spread out among thirty thousand fishing operations, ranging from the single fisherman and his boat, to big corporations running a small fleet. As usual, most of the action was in the Atlantic, where there were some twenty-seven thousand operations, with British Columbia a distant second, with four thousand operations, and the freshwater fishery rounding things out with three thousand. In all, these fishermen were bringing in 2.4 billion pounds of fish each year. Still, the total value of the nation's fishery amounted to less than 0.5 percent of the gross national product.

But beneath the boom was a bust waiting to happen. Canada had gone from a nation of too many fish and not enough good boats, to a country of far too many boats chasing an ever-shrinking resource. The unprecedented catches in the 1960s and 1970s were followed by the all-too-familiar decline and, in some cases, absolute collapse. Canada unilaterally created a two-hundred-mile zone in 1964 and placed severe restrictions on foreign fishermen working within this limit; any fishermen who violate our rules could lose their boats and face heavy fines, and the Department of Fisheries and Oceans (DFO)—the federal agency that oversees our nation's fisheries—was even granted the power to cancel the fishing rights of an entire country. Some of the more naive—and mathematically challenged—politicians believed that this new zone would automatically result in fishermen increasing their catches by two hundred times. It was the same sort of leap of faith that Cabot displayed when he set sail in the *Matthew* for God-knows-where, and it just may be a distinctly Canadian brand of thinking—faith logic—worthy of a book in itself. But the bottom line was that such magical thinking could not save the fishing industry, and most certainly could not save the fish. As recently as 1991, ships from Spain, Portugal and Russia, fishing just outside the two-hundred-mile limit, took one-quarter of the total northern cod catch, breaking every existing treaty. Today, scientists estimate that cod and groundfish stocks are at about 1 percent of their levels from just a decade ago. The fish are giving up the fight, and I think if they had their say, they'd wonder why in God's name anyone would want to celebrate John Cabot's accidental discovery of this land.

Chapter 3

Fishing Rod and the Tyee Pool

Lord, suffer me to catch a fish

So large that even I

When speaking of it afterwards

Have no need to lie.

—"The Angler's Prayer," Anonymous

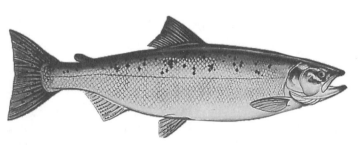

Chinook Salmon

*Discovering that size matters in
Campbell River, B.C.*

y Royal Fishin' Commission began a year before the *Matthew*'s landfall. I'd set off from my house on a rainy Victoria, British Columbia, morning, and headed north. Few stretches of the Trans-Canada Highway are as picturesque, or treacherous, as the section that runs along the east coast of Vancouver Island, snaking its way from Victoria in the south to Port Hardy near the northern tip. Until recently the road was two-lane most of the way, but even nowadays with four lanes for good long stretches, the drive can be a nightmare; the curves are sharp, and even in late July, the rain can be relentless, the fog complete. Not the kind of fog that creeps in on little cat feet: it clomps down like a sick German shepherd and lies there for days. Three and a half hours later, at the mid-point along the Island Highway, sits Campbell River, the self-proclaimed "Salmon Capital of the World" and first stop for my Royal Fishin' Commission.

I arrived in Campbell River in the midst of one of those sick dog fogs, making it hard for me to find my way around. My plan was to meet up with my friend and fishing guru, Lillian Manley, at a place called the Harbourside Cappuccino Bar, squeezed between a Subway and Mike's Barber Shop. The café was part of a brand-new waterfront plaza called Georgia Quay, one of those California-style structures with lots of glass and a green aluminum frame designed to look like oxidized bronze, a reminder that in California and Campbell River, everything new is old again. This quiet Vancouver Island community is in the midst of a building boom; it's one of the fastest-growing communities in the province, thanks to what has become the mantra for Vancouver Island real estate agents and developers, "Hong Kong money." The general belief was that every millionaire in the former British outpost was buying property as a hedge against an uncertain future under Communist China. Like the Klondike Gold Rush one hundred years earlier, "Hong Kong money" sparked a frenzy of economic growth on the Island, to the point where a house in Campbell River—a city that traditionally depends on such unreliable industries as logging and fishing for its economic base—cost more than the same house in downtown Winnipeg or Calgary.

I'd come to Campbell River on Lillian Manley's advice. It was a good starting point because it was one of the rare places in Canada where commercial, sport and native fisheries worked side by side. To Manley's mind, Campbell River was also the place where the image of the Canadian "sportsman" first took shape. "Before Campbell River, Canadian males could be hewers of wood or drawers of water," Manley told me over coffee. "But they could not be men of leisure."

She had a point. The earliest recreational sports for men in this country were hunting, trapping and fishing; men did not feel comfortable simply relaxing, they had to be productive as well. It's an attitude that's persisted to this day.

"Campbell River, thanks to the Tyee Pool and Roderick Haig-Brown, changed all that." Lillian Manley fell silent. She was a curious sort. On the surface, she was outgoing and gregarious, but at the same time she was extremely guarded. I'd known Lillian for seven years, but had no idea what kind of person lurked beneath the eyeliner and rouge. Physically, she was extremely attractive; five foot, seven inches, light build, with aquamarine eyes and a shock of red hair. And while she worked for a living, she didn't really have to. She got an annual allowance provided by the estate of her grandfather, a Welsh coal baron and distant cousin of the writer Gerard Manley Hopkins. The stipend allowed Lillian to indulge in her passion for sportfishing and run her tiny publishing house, which each spring released one or two new fishing books, often written by Lillian herself, as well as her bread-and-butter publication, the *Angler's Monthly Annual*. Lillian despised this magazine because of its focus on the hard-core images of strike, fight and capture. Fish porn, she called it. For her, both commercial fishing and sportfishing were properly seen as contemplative arts, consisting of hours of meditation and rumination occasionally interrupted by the arrival of a fish. She believed that, like the ongoing search for Canadian identity, fishing was a process, not a means to an end, and without that process, fishing as an idea ceased to exist. But what was she to do? *Angler's Monthly Annual* had a huge circulation and ad revenue; it paid the bills. Since I was quite ignorant when it came to fish and fishing, Manley had agreed to lend me her expertise here and there as I travelled east across the country, and I was happy for the helping hand.

We finished our gourmet coffee, got into my car and headed north. Just on the other side of the Campbell River, the town's namesake, we came across a quaint bed and breakfast with a curious name: the Haig-Brown Kingfisher Creek Heritage Property. To the uninitiated, it was hardly worth a second glance, but to anglers the world over, it's a hallowed shrine to Roderick Haig-Brown, the pre-eminent fishing writer of his generation, if not the century. Haig-Brown called the house Above Tide because it was built at the first point on the river beyond the reach of the highest of high tides. I had not seen the place in twenty-five years, but it was much as I remembered it. Although the property is overrun now with bracken, fern and bushes, the green lawn remains, well-trimmed, flowing from the patio one hundred yards back to the river. I could imagine distant Sunday afternoons on this lawn, as family and friends gathered for a game of croquet in the cool heat of west coast summer.

Manley took my picture standing at the front door of Above Tide, holding my rod, a fierce, manly look on my face. Just being there brought back a flood of memories, and I was swept back to the moment I first met Haig-Brown. It was the summer of 1971, and my Scout troop had made a pilgrimage to his house. He often welcomed such visitors to his home, believing that it was important to share his love of nature and the local rivers, and he had a soft spot for Boy Scouts, his godfather having been none other than the organization's founder, Lord Baden-Powell. Haig-Brown was a lean man, slightly stiff although still agile; he clenched a pipe between his teeth as he demonstrated the proper fly-casting technique, although he always removed it before he spoke in his modulated English accent. I'd never before seen a man of his generation in jeans, but that's what he wore: well-used jeans and a faded work shirt. Despite his curious dress, I knew instantly that he was a man full of the authority that came with experience and knowledge, a man not without warmth, but who was capable of a sudden look so cold, to steal poet Al Purdy's words, it could chill beer. What impressed me most about Haig-Brown was his confidence in the woods. The nine little members of my Scout pack practised making fires out of sticks and mending broken limbs with leaves and branches, and we took our weekend camping trips at Goldstream Provincial Park, but the truth was we were terrified of the forest, all of us, to a man, right down to the slightly cross-eyed, slightly bow-legged accountant Mr. Finch, our Scout leader. Beneath Haig-Brown's aristocratic veneer beat the heart of a woodsman who was, unlike most of us native-born Canadians, as comfortable in the forest as he was in his own backyard.

Roderick Langmere Haig-Brown was born at 6:15 in the morning on February 21, 1908, at Stratton Cottage, Shoreham-by-the-Sea, Sussex, England, to proud parents Alan, a teacher, and Violet, whose family made beer and money. The baby Roderick weighed in at seven and a half pounds, and at twenty-one inches long, he was definitely a keeper.

When Roderick was ten, his father was killed in the Great War; two years later the boy, his mother and two sisters moved into the mansion of beer baron Alfred Pope, his maternal grandfather, where Roderick developed into a lacklustre student and exceptional athlete, particularly keen on shooting and angling, favourite pastimes of the Edwardian gentleman. At his grandfather's house, Roderick was immersed in the British sportsman's ethic—an unwritten code that stressed, with schoolboy charm, the values of fair play, knowledge, self-discipline, self-respect. While the sportsman's ethic guided Haig-Brown's behaviour in field and stream, at school it was another matter. He rebelled against the rigid authority and at sixteen, after slipping off to London with some friends for a night of drinking and partying, rowdy Roddy Haig-Brown was expelled from the very school where his paternal grandfather had once been headmaster. Two years later he took his university entrance exams but decided to take a job offer from a family friend who ran a logging business in Washington State. When his visa ran out, Roderick moved to the Nimpkish Valley, west of Campbell River, where he worked as a logger, trapper, commercial fisherman and guide. One of his friends was the legendary tracker Cougar Smith, who killed six hundred mountain lions in his career as a bounty hunter, and who finished his days working as a fishing guide out of Painter's Lodge. After three years in the bush, Haig-Brown went back to England, but in 1931 he realized that lurking beneath his Edwardian surface was the soul of a Canadian. "I might go elsewhere,"

he wrote in the posthumously released *Writings and Reflections,*
"but my heart would settle for nowhere else." What Haig-Brown
fell in love with was less a nation than a notion, a "continuously
expanding idea"; although Canada was, and remains, largely
urban, Haig-Brown was attracted to its wilderness where rugged
individuals could survive and even thrive by following the sportsman's code. Above all, Canada was the place where disenfran-
chised men like Haig-Brown could break free from the rigid
British class system and leave their mark on the world. "It's good
to be writing at the start of a country's history instead of at the
end," Haig-Brown wrote in 1950. "There is no limiting tradition
at such a time, no need for precious form or pretty experiment.
There is only subject, too vast to be seen clearly, too amorphous
to be pressed into completely recognizable shape."

Haig-Brown spent the last forty years of his life in Campbell
River, where he served as town magistrate, not because he had any
legal training but, as he later explained to Al Purdy, because he
was the "only guy in town with time and education for the job."
When he wasn't in court, Haig-Brown could be found either fishing on the rivers or writing in his study at Above Tide. He tried
his hand at several literary forms—animal stories, juvenile fiction,
novels, histories—but it's through his fishing books that he earned
an international reputation. His stories and articles appeared in
The New Yorker, Field and Stream, Saturday Night and countless
other magazines, while his fishing books—starting with *The Western Angler* in 1939, right up to *To Know a River,* published twenty
years after his 1976 death—were as popular in England and the
United States as they are at home. Although he's forever linked in
the popular imagination with the monsters of the Tyee Pool, Haig-
Brown was not a member of the Tyee Club and took no pleasure
in "that regimented and competitive kind of fishing," just as he
had taken no pleasure in the regimented, competitive life of the

English schoolboy. His medium was fly-fishing, and he was an expert with the dry fly, long considered the angler's highest art form. "It is undoubtedly the best and finest of all forms of fishing," Haig-Brown wrote in his *Primer of Fly-Fishing*, and added that the "natural development of any fisherman, except possibly the big-game fisherman, is toward fly-fishing."

What exactly are the various levels an angler can ascend to? What distinguishes the "dry-fly" fishing aficionado from the dope with the ten-dollar tackle from Sears? According to Lillian Manley, trolling is the lowest rung on the sport fisherman's evolutionary ladder, and easily the most popular form of fishing, particularly on the ocean or deep-water lakes. Not to be confused with trawling, which is something commercial fishermen do with a net, trolling simply means pulling the hooked line behind a boat. It's a very effective way to catch fish and results in the hook being well-set in the fish's mouth, but no matter how you dress it up it's an ugly way to fish. Haig-Brown himself refused to troll as a matter of principle.

On the next rung we find spin-casting. Any kid who's ever fished will be familiar with this kind of gear, which is based on a mechanical reel engaged by the press of a button. This means that virtually anyone can master the lowest form of casting in a matter of minutes. The rod and reel are usually packaged together at an affordable price. Bait-casting comes next, and although it is considered the most difficult kind of angling to master, it's still rather ungainly. The bait-casting lure has a revolving spool, which is a dangerous weapon in the hands of anything less than a supreme fishing being. The spool has a tendency to spin faster than the line, and often knots up on the reel, causing an unexpected backlash of bait and hook. Finally, we hit fly-fishing, which, like its distant cousin the martini, is divided into wet and dry. Both use a special reel that is good for reeling in the line but can't draw it out like a casting reel does. Anglers have to hand-draw their line before releasing it. Wet flies are heavier and sink below the water surface; the fish usually takes them as the angler reels in. Dry flies are lighter and stay on the surface. Anglers must use every ounce of their skill to make the dry fly look and act as realistic as possible.

While fish and fishing were Haig-Brown's obsessions, he was fascinated with his adopted country and its people. Originally, Canada appealed to the child in him, just as his writing would later appeal to the child in his readers. His vision of this country came from tall tales he heard in the schoolyard and the animal adventure stories of Charles Roberts and Ernest Thompson Seton. Haig-Brown arrived in this country with his head full of "rumors and old wives' tales." In the essay "Coastscape," which originally appeared in *Maclean's*, he says that he imagined the typical Canadian as "a tall, lean man, quiet-spoken, keen-eyed, totally dependable in any crisis or tough undertaking." Haig-Brown quickly changed his mind.

All Canadians were not tall, nor were they calm and laconic; many were small and voluble, most were hard, driving workers through the day and loved to talk in the bunkhouses at night; to be catty—quick and sure on one's feet—was a virtue far beyond mere strength. To use one's brains and ingenuity in the moving of bulk and weight—huge logs, whole trees, donkey engines on sleds, crippled locomotives— was the supreme virtue. Few of my companions were woodsmen, though those few were highly skilled. Most considered anything beyond the edge of the logging slash dangerous and mysterious territory.

Despite his aversion to the Tyee Pool, Haig-Brown did not undermine the Campbell River myth. He built on that myth, and it in turn enhanced the Haig-Brown legend. He became the voice from the wilderness, whose warm but meticulous writing unwittingly declared that civilization had arrived even in this remote corner of the world. At the same time, he elevated the status of sportfishing from a simple leisure activity to a contemplative art that was a semi-productive way for a Canadian man to spend his time. All this was lost on me as a child. To me Haig-Brown was simply a magical figure, an ageless wilderness sage. The fish were our responsibility, he told us repeatedly as he drilled us on the fine points of fly-casting in his backyard. As it turned out, I was as hopeless an angler on dry land as I would prove to be on water. I did manage to knock Haig-Brown's pipe out of his mouth on my forward swing. He stoically picked the pipe up and offered me some calm words of encouragement before putting it back in his mouth. Later, I managed to stick a hook in Mr. Finch's pants, perilously close to his crotch.

Despite our generally poor showing on the lawn, Haig-Brown agreed to take us to his favourite fishing spot several miles up Campbell River. While I can remember only the kind of details that stick in the mind of a twelve-year-old boy—my brother Greg wandered into a patch of stinging nettles and later got a rash shaped like Jupiter on his back; some fat kid whose name I can't remember, who might have been Mr. Finch's son, somehow got stung on the tongue by a mud wasp—I do recall being impressed by Haig-Brown's complete understanding of the river. He seemed to read it like a book, and along the way pointed out interesting passages to this troop of earnest nincompoops.

After a long walk through the brush, which left us feeling completely at Haig-Brown's mercy, we arrived at a still pool protected on one side by a sharp curve in the river and, on the other, by an enormous cedar stump. Even in the last days of summer, the pool was deep and black. Haig-Brown stood by the water's edge and went over some of our earlier lesson, and spoke of the habits of the steelhead salmon, how they favoured fast-flowing water with a gravel bottom for spawning, and cool pools such as this to laze away a summer afternoon. Fish, Haig-Brown said with a straight face, were not much different from boys.

For some reason known only to God and Haig-Brown, I was selected to demonstrate casting technique. Haig-Brown handed me the rod and talked me through the sequence. My first attempt landed a couple of feet forward, several feet to the right. My second try actually hit the nearest edge of the pool. I threw my body and soul into the third cast, and it dropped almost without the smallest splash at the very centre of the pool. The master was about to congratulate me on a job well done, when a figure rose from the black and took my fly solidly. She jumped almost as soon as the hook was home, and I saw that bright flash of silver come clear out of the water and land with a slap on her side. For once, there was a crack in Haig-Brown's armour. "It's a coho, and a good one too," he said in a deliberate voice that could not conceal his amazement. "Let her run." I tried to hand the rod to Haig-Brown, but he passed me a beer-chilling look; this fish was my responsibility. The first run took her fifteen yards away, moving so quickly I was sure she'd already thrown the hook, and so close to the surface I could see her eyes. Suddenly, the fish turned back towards me, then jumped three times in succession. "Keep reeling," Haig-Brown said, his voice as deep and calm as the pool. Finally, I got the better of the fish. I began to reel towards the bank. "Steady," Haig-Brown cautioned. "You're going to have to beach her." The fish was barely arm's length away. I paused for an instant, readying myself for one final reel. In that moment, the fish spat the fly. With a speed and suddenness as frightening as death, she was gone.

I was afraid to look at Haig-Brown.

When I did raise my eyes, I saw his broad smile, as big as the fish I'd caught and lost, teeth stained almost brown from years of pipe tobacco. "Absolutely excellent effort," he said, patting my shoulder. "You'll make a fine angler some day." When we got back to Above Tide, Haig-Brown presented me with one of his personal flies, called a silver-bodied bucktail, if my memory serves me. It's a childhood memento that I cherish to this day. Well. I would cherish it, if I hadn't traded it one week later for an autographed picture of Jacques Plante, my all-time favourite goalie.

I find it interesting that the older Haig-Brown got, the less inclined he was to fish. In his final years, he set down the rod and reel and took up the mask and snorkel. He preferred to spend his days swimming among the spawning salmon, mesmerized by their purposeful, fatal activity. This was the final stage in Haig-Brown's evolution: shed of all his literary disguises, the swimmer. It was a logical progression. Over time, he'd become an outspoken conservationist, publicly opposing the proliferation of hydroelectric dams and pulp mills in this "last corner of the west." He'd recognized early in his life that the wild was not to be feared, nor harnessed, nor subdued. "I love the yield of the Canadian land and water," he wrote in *Writings and Reflections*. "It is on this and from this that the people of Canada, directly or indirectly, have their being. It is in searching out the land, learning to live in it, learning to use it, that we have been shaped and tempered."

Lillian and I spent the last few hours of Campbell River sunlight strolling the Above Tide grounds, then returned to the car for a short ride due east. One mile down the road, we came to a busy collection of buildings nestled on the edge of Discovery Passage. It was Painter's Lodge, the most famous fishing resort in the country. Originally built by Ned Painter in the height of the Depression, the lodge had been completely rebuilt after a fire on Christmas Eve, 1985.

I parked the car, then we made our way through the lobby of the resort, past the gourmet restaurant, and, reluctantly, the bar. We stopped for a moment in the foyer to admire some of the photographs and memorabilia on display. Bob Hope, Glenn Ford, John Wayne, the Marx Brothers all made their way to the resort in its heyday—even the King of Siam came to find the King of Salmon. I lingered over the pictures of those fortunate few who'd managed to land, in the language of the lodge, a "button fish," those fish big enough to earn the lucky angler a commemorative pin from the local Tyee Club. There was M.E. Charleston, whose 52-pounder in 1924 netted him the Tyee Club's First Man of the Year award; Mrs. W.C. Butler, in fur collar and formal hat, standing beside her 60-pound catch; Ray Slocum and his 70.5-pound tyee, which set a club record when it was caught in 1947; Walter Shutts, who broke that record in 1968 with a 71-pounder; Colin Munn, whose 63.6-pounder set the standard for the 1990s. In every photo, the expressions are the same. The anglers gleam. The fish, suspended by its tail, hangs upside down, eyes wide open, mouth agape. But what I found more interesting than the photos themselves was Lillian's face as she pored over them. Her characteristic cool was gone; her eyes lit up, ignited by the thought of hooking in to one of these giant fish.

After checking in, we wandered to the docks just beyond the edge of the trimmed lawn. Standing on the wharf, I could see

Boston Whalers come and go, carrying tourists in their yellow suits, out for a day's fishing. While the mandate of Painter's Lodge has changed in recent years, and it now caters more to families and business clients than to the trophy fishermen of the world, it has a tremendous history behind it and, most important, the Tyee Pool in front of it. This is a fishing hole, no bigger than a hockey rink, that runs along the outside of a sand spit at the point where the Campbell River meets the ocean, a spot where spawning chinook salmon gather before beginning their arduous journey up river. One of the guides, a congenial fellow named Mark, pointed the spot out to me, and as we watched half a dozen rowboats jockey for position on the Tyee Pool I recalled what Lillian Manley had said about it that morning over coffee. "It's there that anglers come in search of the legendary tyee, king of all salmon." She spoke with the kind of forced dramatic tone she liked to adopt at moments like this. "It's there that the idea of this country took the form and shape of a fish."

Not a separate species, as some think, tyee is an honorary title bestowed on chinook salmon of thirty or more pounds, the kind of salmon that return year after year to the mouth of Campbell River. The word *chinook* means "chief" in the language of the Chinook people, expert merchants based at the mouth of the Columbia River, whose language became the pidgin English of native traders up and down the west coast. Thanks to the Chinooks, we also have the marvellous "skookum," a B.C. version of "awesome, dude." Campbell River isn't the only place where big chinook salmon are found—a record 126-pounder was netted in southeastern Alaska—but they seem to occur in far greater numbers there than anywhere else in the world. The secret probably lies in the river bed. Chinook lay their eggs in gravel, but in this particular river, the bottom is made up of fairly large stones called cobble rock; it takes a

56

big fish to properly prepare her nest, and over time natural selection has taken place.

It's these big fish that put Campbell River on the sportsman's map. As far back as one hundred years ago, word of the monstrous tyee had reached Mother England, and genteel Edwardian sportsmen spared no effort to get to Campbell River. These guys were used to catching Atlantic salmon, which rarely weighed more than fifteen pounds. But they weren't surprised to discover these Pacific monsters; a land as big and wild as Canada would be expected to produce such a wondrous fish. And of course, being men—as Lillian was quick to point out—they could only assume that bigger was better. Lillian directed me to an article that appeared in the October 28, 1896, edition of the popular "country gentleman's newspaper," *The Field*. It reported a "salmon fishing expedition" led by Sir Richard Musgrave, and includes a certain Mr. W. Tayleur's account of battling a sixty-eight-pound tyee.

I felt I was into a big one; a whirr, and away he went straight for the sea, both Indians paddling for their lives. But no good, he gained on us too fast, until my line was actually run clean out, and I gave him the point in order that he should break the cast and not the rod top, but he was slacking a bit now, and gradually I raised my point higher and higher until, at length, I was enabled to get a turn at my wheel, and inch by inch fight for some line. I had recovered about fifteen yards, when away he went again, this time running some distance along the top of the water and throwing himself madly into the air. Good heavens! What a monster! My Indians gave a deep gurgle of delight, but we were at it again and soon out to sea where the Indians managed the canoe magnificently in the choppy water. All the time, the fish was hard at work, one

57

moment running for life, the next diving to the deepest depths: again, rising like a flash to the surface, rolling and tumbling over and fighting like a Trojan, straining my Castleconnell rod almost to breaking point. But there was little fear of a break, although it was bent double. With such pressure, no fish could live much longer, and he had the butt for the best part of an hour. His rushes grew feebler and feebler, and now I could stop and manage him. At last I had him on the surface, so beat he could hardly turn over.

Not only is it one of the earliest incidences of product placement on record—note Tayleur's use of the fishing rod brand name—but it's also the earliest Canadian fish porn on record. In any case, the five members of the Musgrave expedition netted a hundred fish, with a total weight of more than three thousand pounds. Reports of their success put Campbell River on the sportsman's map, while reinforcing the Old World image of Canada as an endless wilderness—complete with colourful natives catering to the master's every whim—of limitless bounty. Why all the fuss? According to Manley, the turn-of-the-century sportsmen considered these tyee just a variation of their familiar Atlantic salmon. In fact, while there is only a single species of Atlantic salmon, there are eleven species of Pacific salmon, including chinook, chum, coho, pink, sockeye (and its landlocked, freshwater equivalent, kokanee); cutthroat, golden and Apache trout; and the Asian cousins, masu and amago. While Atlantic and Pacific salmon share many traits, they differ in one major respect; the former may spawn several times in its life, while the latter, with the exception of the steelhead, spawns once and dies. Here was Nature at her most brutal, where the act of procreation was suicide itself. In fact, the image was too powerful for the European imagination. The early settlers refused to accept the annual spectacle of sex and death, and considered the tales of absolute destruction an Indian myth. Surely God, in His infinite wisdom, would allow some salmon to survive?

According to Lillian Manley, the sportsmen of the world lost interest in Campbell River's great fish as the century progressed, and perhaps the image of the tyee would have slipped into obscurity if it hadn't been for the vision of a man known in fishing circles as the Lone Angler. J.A. Wiborn was a doctor from California and friend of the writer Zane Grey, who'd given him his nickname and written about him in dozens of books and articles. In 1923, Wiborn joined Grey for a trek to the Tyee Pool, and the doctor immediately saw its economic potential. He joined forces with Melville Haigh, the bank-appointed manager of the financially troubled Willows Hotel, and A.N. Wolverton, a devoted angler from Vancouver, and together the three men started the Tyee Club. They saw the organization as a means to both protect salmon stocks and give Campbell River's salmon—already in decline because of sports and commercial overfishing—a much-needed shot in the fin.

Using California's Catalina Tuna Club as a model, Wiborn's first step was to regulate tackle. While the Tyee Pool had been attracting the sportsmen of the world, many were not above bending the rules of fair play to the breaking point, using short, strong rods with little play, and heavy-duty reels that provided enough drag to, in the words of one observer, "stop a buffalo." In fact, a study done in 1922 indicated that seven out of eight anglers were fishing with handlines, heavy-duty hand-held lines adapted from commercial fishing. Often, they'd tie the handline to a boat or cedar block, which the hooked fish dragged around Discovery

Passage until they passed out from exhaustion. So along with regulations for rods and reels, the Tyee Club imposed severe restrictions on lines. Before nylon, the best fishing line was made from intertwined linen strings, called strands. The Tyee Club had a nine-strand maximum, equal to what anglers call a twenty-five-pound test, that is, line that can withstand up to twenty-five pounds of pressure in a controlled test.

Equipment alone did not qualify anglers for membership in the Tyee Club. First, they had to land a chinook of thirty pounds or more. Successful candidates were awarded pins, colour-coded to the salmon's weight: a thirty- to forty-pound tyee earned a bronze pin; a forty- to fifty-pounder, silver; right on up to a ruby pin for fish seventy pounds or more. There was more than a hint of elitism behind the club, which probably accounted for its unqualified success. Even as the shadow of the Great Depression fell across the Western world, Campbell River's sportfishing industry shone. For the most part, these anglers lived above the realm of money. They were bankers and businessmen and captains of industry, with the odd movie star and prince thrown in for good measure. It was common for anglers to leave their guides with a hundred-dollar tip, a staggering sum of money in a town where the average logger or seiner would come home at the end of a long day with two dollars in his pocket.

Enter Ned Painter, an enterprising boat-builder from Vancouver. He showed up in Campbell River just as the fishing was hitting its peak. He had a great idea: he would build his durable rowboats all winter, rent them out to anglers in the peak seasons, then sell them off at the end of the year. His plan was an instant success, and Painter soon found that the anglers who came to rent his boats were more and more demanding. In those days, the only place to stay in town was the Willows Hotel, a loggers' saloon that Zane Grey described as "a strange mixture of civilization and discomfort." Ned Painter's well-heeled and often high-heeled guests soon tired of the Willows, and begged him to provide some accommodation closer to the action. At first, he set tents up on wood platforms, then in 1930 he built nine cottages. The guests wanted more. Finally, in 1938, Painter built the lodge that would become famous the world over.

Why did the Campbell River tyee become part of the lifestyle of the Depression's rich and famous? On the surface it seems simple enough; wealthy anglers came to the Tyee Pool to test their skill and strength against these mighty fish. It was just another example of the kind of commercial exploitation that underlies Canadian history, with the wealthy and connected presuming that the country's natural bounty was theirs for the taking. But Manley believes there was more to it. "The fish were actually secondary to the experience," she said. "Most anglers didn't keep their catch; the fish were usually given to the guides, who'd sell them for five cents a pound to the Quathiaski Cannery on Quadra Island."

For Manley, the tyee had an important symbolic value. Campbell River represented British Columbia in the popular imagination, and at that time many saw this province as North America's final frontier, "the last corner of the west," as Roderick Haig-Brown wrote. It was the moment in history when "wilderness" was moving from fact to fancy: at the turn of the century, only 30 percent of Canada's population lived in urban centres; by 1921, that number had climbed to 50 percent. In the face of such rapid urbanization—and in the midst of an unbroken chain of war and economic turmoil—Manley believed that Canadians looked to Campbell River and its wondrous salmon as an enduring image of the past. "In reality, we had already subdued nature, but through

this almost ritualized sacrifice of the tyee salmon, we could perpet-
uate the central Canadian myth of Man against the Wilderness."

I stood on the dock behind Painter's Lodge in the fading daylight
and thought of Haig-Brown. He was the first great angler this
country produced, and, along with the tyee of Campbell River, he
helped create the image of the Canadian-male-as-sportsman that
persists to this day. Sportfishing continues to be a thriving industry, particularly on Canada's freshwater lakes and streams, which
are home to 90 percent of this country's anglers. Unlike trap-
pers—who co-exist in relative peace with recreational hunters—
anglers and commercial fishermen don't see eye to eye. Each
blames the other for undermining the resource, while both point
accusing fingers at the small native food fishery. But I'm reluctant
to draw too big a distinction between commercial and recreational
fishing in this country. People already tend to compartmentalize
the two industries, as if neither had an impact on the other. Fish
are fish. It doesn't matter if they're caught by gillnet, purse seine,
down-rigger, or a ball of twine with a bent diaper pin—it's impossible to appreciate the turmoil in our fishery without considering
the major groups vying for the resource.

In the meantime, Haig-Brown's worst nightmares have been
realized. Thanks to decades of sports and commercial overfishing
and the ongoing pollution and destruction of spawning habitats by
forest companies and hydroelectric plants, Campbell River's fish
stocks are dwindling. For sports anglers on the Pacific coast there
are gear restrictions, fishing closures and strict limits: in season,
there's a four-salmon daily limit. However, the community plugs
on, selling itself, as it always has, as a natural wonder, a wilderness
experience, with fine dining and health club included. Rather than

staying for a month at a time, tourists now come for a weekend and supplement their fishing with whale-watching tours and day trips to Nootka Sound; there's even a company called Campbell River Snorkel Tours, which will set you up for a day with a wet suit, mask and snorkel, to swim with the fish making their way up the river.

And you can still fish. The Tyee Pool is closed to motorboats from July 15 to September 15, and for fifty dollars an hour Painter's Lodge will rent you a rowboat, gear and guide included. Or you can head a few miles north to Seymour Narrows, and try your luck with pinks, chum and coho, but for anyone who cares about the fish, it's a double-edged sword: the good news is you caught a fish; the bad news? You caught a fish.

It was already dark, the sun disappearing quickly behind the Campbell River's mountain backdrop. I searched the sky for shooting stars and listened to the tethered boats rise and brush against the wharfs. There was a cool night breeze, typical for the time of the year, and that Pacific Ocean stink—a mix of salt, cedar and rotting seaweed—was unusually sharp. Manley and I had an early day ahead of us; the manager of Painter's Lodge had kindly offered us a rowboat and tackle to try our luck in the Tyee Pool first thing in the morning. Then I was off to Ladner on the mainland for the second stop on my Royal Fishin' Commission, and Manley was heading to New Zealand in search of the legendary giant pygmy groper.

She had already turned in, and I was about to follow, when out of the corner of my eye I saw something dart past the dock, and when I scanned the water I spotted a large chinook salmon weaving through the support posts. I'd seen fry that close to shore before, but never a full-grown fish. Then another salmon swam by, and another, and suddenly the water boiled with them, thousands and thousands of fish, flipping their tails at me as they swam past, taunting me to catch them. The tide was high, but even so, the water could not have been more than ten feet deep. Soon, the salmon were stacked up, one on top of the other, so many of them swirling around that I could actually see them bump heads; I imagined jumping from fish to fish as if they were stepping stones. I scanned the wharf and spotted a net leaning against the gutting table. I glanced around to make sure the coast was clear, then grabbed the net and got down on my knees. It's not strictly legal to net a living, healthy, free-swimming salmon. In fact, it's quite illegal. But fish—like love and tax assessments—can drive men to desperate acts, and, as anyone who's failed their entire life to catch a fish will understand, I slipped the net into the water and slid it into the path of an oncoming chinook.

The fish swam right past my net and seemed to glance towards me as if he could not believe the pathetic depths to which I had sunk.

So I lay down the net and I did something I had never done before, something few people ever get to do outside an aquarium or fish farm. I watched the salmon swim around. I watched with interest, without malice or purpose, and wondered what the fish were doing, swimming one direction then another like a giant, sequinned puppy chasing its tail, always turning at the same moment, as if they shared the same mind or, at least, the same intent. And, as I watched, I was overcome with—I don't know what to call it. Ecstasy? Rapture? I can only describe it as a kind of spiritual invigoration, a joy swirling around inside me, bumping into itself. It was a sensation I'd experienced only once before, when I was playing goal for the Racquet Club Bantam House B team and was knocked out cold by a slap shot to the temple. These were the two most spiritually profound moments in my life, which proves either:

(a) The Lord works in mysterious ways; or,

(b) I don't get out of the house enough.

In any case, the fish had eluded me yet again, but I had a funny feeling, deep down inside, that this time they were trying to send me a message, and perhaps, just maybe, my luck was about to change.

Presumably, it would be for the better.

The Obligatory Catch Scene

Suddenly the tip jerked downward. Silence. Lillian Manley nodded, indicating that I should take my rod out of its holder. "If she goes," Manley cautioned, "remember to give a sharp pull, and release the line from the down-rigger."

Several agonizing seconds passed, but the rod remained rigid, straining, it seemed, to flex itself to its fullest and gain every advantage over our unseen quarry. Manley shrugged and was about to speak when my rod jerked again, with greater force than before. I gave a quick pull to release the line and the fight was on.

"Let her go," Manley said grimly as she furiously reeled in her own line. She did not want to lose another fish.

My reel spun in a frenzy, and with every metre of line taken, the tension mounted, the rod arched further. "Keep your tip up!" Manley implored, and I fought to raise it out of the salt chuck. When I gained on the fish, Manley let out a shout.

"Now!" she cried. "Set the hook now!"

I braked the reel with my thumb and took hold of the handle. All at once, I began to reel in. My rod lunged forward as the line stiffened. For a moment, I expected it to snap or at least relax, the great fish beneath me having thrown its hook. But the hook set. I reeled in for a few moments, then let her take the line. But I was not prepared for what happened next. The line went slack.

"She's coming back on you," Manley warned. "Keep reeling." Her voice was calm but assertive. With a resolute flick of her wrist, she cut the engine. She had made up her mind that I was going to land this fish.

I reeled furiously until the line began to tighten, but to my surprise the fish seemed to give no resistance.

"I think I've lost her," I said.

Manley's expression did not change. "Keep reeling."

I tried several more turns, but the fish did not put up a fight. I lowered my arms, disheartened with the realization that I'd lost another. But the reel spun off again. I let her play a little, then began to wind in. The line twisted and turned with such violence that I was sure I would lose her, but all at once, she broke surface ten metres from our rowboat. It was a spawning chinook, and a good-sized one at that, perhaps even a button fish. She came three-quarters of the way out of the water, then turned on her side, loudly slapping the surface as she descended. I kept reeling until the fish was in clear sight, and Manley readied the net. I'd come this far, but knew that we were approaching the most critical point; this is where the fight is won or lost, where the final struggle between man and nature is decided.

Manley dipped the net into the water, as the fish zigzagged only a few metres away. The fish rolled over several times in succession, a last desperate attempt to escape, but now her cause seemed lost, the gaping net within arm's length. All at once she dropped, then lunged forward. In an instant my line went slack. I watched my adversary turn tail and swim downward to safety.

"Shit," I said, in a voice barely audible.

"Shit indeed," Manley echoed. "Shit indeed . . ."

Chapter 4

Fish and Ships

. . . . You have reached
a town of infinite distances where the night
whispers "nothing is gained by going with
the current." This is the final welcome.
From here you're on your own.

— "Ladner," Tim Bowling

Sockeye Salmon

Trawling for truth and salmon in
Ladner, B.C.

A late August rainstorm had hit Vancouver, and I was stuck in stop-and-go traffic on the approach to the George Massey Tunnel. I was in the middle of what residents of the Lower Mainland euphemistically term the afternoon "rush hour." In fact, it's more like three hours, and you do anything but rush. Welcome to Vancouver, home to the slowest commute in the country, where the typical working man or woman spends one-eighth of their waking life driving to and from work.

The problem is that the city has gotten too big for its bridges. During the 1960s and 1970s, the population remained stable, but during the 1980s, as central Canada was hit hard by the recession, Vancouver opened its arms and economy to Asian Pacific markets. The population boomed, growing by almost half a million in a single decade. Right now, there's almost two million people living in the basin surrounding the lower part of the Fraser River, and planners expect this number to increase another third over the next three decades. This growth will put a tremendous strain on a region that's already stretched to the limits. Few people actually live in the city, and to get to the residential areas most people have to traverse either Burrard Inlet to the north, or one of the arms of the Fraser River to the south. The result is a huge increase in the volume of traffic, served by a woefully outdated network of roads and bridges and exactly one tunnel.

Time, as Lillian Manley liked to remind me, was of the essence. To meet heavy scheduling constraints, I'd budgeted only one day for this leg of my Royal Fishin' Commission, and as I reached the mouth of the George Massey Tunnel I had only two hours left. The traffic near the tunnel entrance is always heavy in the late afternoon. Here, cars from the Steveston Highway merge onto the main road, Highway 99, producing an intricate bottleneck, which, I imagine, must be viewed from space to be truly appreciated. Stuck in this spot, I watched as a tug led a huge freighter over the tunnel, along the Fraser River, one of the best-known commercial waterways in the country. The river is an access route for the political and economic expansion of Canada, serving first the fur trade and a gold rush, before settling down as a highway for timber and freight. Most lower mainlanders, even those who live right on its shore, don't even realize that the Fraser is home to one of the most productive fisheries on earth.

The Fraser's source lay some 820 miles away from this traffic jam, in a collection of mountain springs and streams by the Alberta border. Along the way, it winds through the heart of the province: Prince George, Quesnel, Williams Lake, Lillooet, Lytton, where the Fraser joins with the Thompson River, Hope, where Sylvester Stallone made his first Rambo film, New Westminster, the former provincial capital, where the river splits in two, and finally, past Vancouver to the fertile delta built up by the river over ten thousand years. Along the way, the Fraser collects silt and sewage and storm-drain runoff, pesticides and chemical fertilizers from farms and orchards, effluent from pulp mills and God knows what other industrial waste, gasoline and fuel oils from the freighters, tugs, fish boats and pleasure craft that crowd its waters. One recent study suggests that as many as 90 percent of all the fish in the Fraser River suffered from one or more physical irregularities, most likely a result of pollution. But this was no surprise to biologists familiar with the Fraser. The alarm bells started going off back in the summer of 1993, when as many as two dozen Fraser River white sturgeon mysteriously washed up on shore over the course of a few weeks. These prehistoric creatures can live more than one hundred years, growing up to eleven feet long and weighing more than six hundred pounds. Despite their size, they're particularly vulnerable; they're more than just bottom feeders, they live in muck on the river bed, often passing years in the same spot, their bodies exposed to every kind of poison and pollution the mighty river has to offer.

The exit just after the tunnel is River Road, and it took me right into Ladner, the second stop on my national tour. Once, when this area was accessible only by the Lulu Island ferry, Ladner was an isolated fishing and farming community. But things changed after the highway went in in 1959, and although you still see fish boats moored at the government wharf, the village has become a bedroom community. Where it once helped feed the world, Ladner now feeds Vancouver's insatiable craving for barely affordable family housing. It's a place with lots of strip malls and condo developments—like Westham Lane, with one-bedrooms starting at $149,000—and where family restaurants outnumber the fast-food joints five to one.

It was a homecoming of sorts for me. After graduating from university in 1981, I was faced with the bleak prospect of finding a job. The recession was just starting and there wasn't much work out there for a PhysEd major, with a minor in Canadian literature, and like most of my classmates, I was forced to explore opportunities outside my area of expertise. Since forestry dominates British Columbia's economy—generating about $10 billion each year, and providing jobs for 35 percent of the labour force—a lot of my friends found work as loggers, as we call lumberjacks on the west coast, as pulp mill workers or with the survey crews that map and catalogue British Columbia's forest inventories. Others found jobs in construction or the service industry, waiting tables or slinging beer while a few got hired on as deckhands with the fish boats. It was an enviable job. You could clear five or six thousand dollars over the season, and, if you played your cards right, still get in enough days to qualify for UIC. I was one of the lucky ones. My uncle Roger owned a thirty-six-foot gillnetter that he kept moored at the government wharf in Ladner, and he invited me to come work for him at fifty dollars a day plus a cut of the profits at the end of the season.

I had some reservations about working with my uncle. Physically, he fit my romantic image of an old salt: his long hair, bleached white by the sun, a dirty aura; a perpetual bristle of beard on his chin; a wardrobe consisting of exactly one pair of overalls and two denim work shirts. My brothers and I called him Jolly Roger behind his back, a nickname that only partly reflected his true character: he was "jolly" for only about two hours every day, starting just after the hangover subsided, and ending soon after his morning coffee wore off. And even then, he was "jolly" in only the loosest sense of the word. He might, for example, look up from his crossword when he spoke to you, or, on those rare occasions when he engaged in conversation, remember your name. But I needed the money, and decided to take a chance. I signed aboard with Uncle Roger and the ragtag crew of the *Barabas II*, and moved to Ladner to begin my career as a commercial fisherman on the Fraser River.

Over thousands and thousands of years, silt has built up at the mouth of the mighty Fraser, creating a fertile plain that encompasses much of what we now call the Lower Mainland. It's marvellous farmland—that's what first attracted settlers to areas like Ladner—but it's the last place on earth you'd want to be when an earthquake strikes. Much of the land will simply liquefy when the Big One comes—and believe me, it's coming. But the first settlers weren't thinking about earthquakes. They came to farm and quickly realized the value of the fishery that flowed past their doors. In 1877, Jim Laidlaw, Frank Page and Joe Lyons opened the Delta Canning Company, near the site of the new government wharf, and other canneries soon followed. Commercial fishing on the Fraser didn't start with the Europeans; the natives had fished the waters for thousands of years, and one fish in particular, the oolichan, was at the heart of a commercial trade network that ran the length of the west coast, from Alaska to Oregon, and as far east as the Rocky Mountains. The natives processed this small smelt to extract the rich grease, which they prized for its taste and medicinal powers.

The earliest traders in British Columbia established their posts near major spawning grounds like the Fraser and, to the north, the Skeena River, and bartered with the natives for fish as well as furs. And as early as 1835, west coast fishermen were exporting salt-cured salmon to places as far off as Hawaii. But it was the 1858 Fraser River Gold Rush that created a local market for salmon, and as gold fever faded, people looked to other resources to pick up the slack. There wasn't too much around. But there were a lot of forests, and there were a lot of fish. Gold had brought the world to British Columbia, and in a smaller way, these fish brought Ladner to the world, and a way of life to the people of Ladner. At first, the Ladner fishermen found that the rewards barely outweighed the risks. The local canneries supplied them with gear and twenty-foot skiffs, some rigged for sailing, some not, then sent them off to do battle with the river. Many died when their boats were overcome by the flow, the tide or the wind. In return for risking their lives, the fishermen earned seven cents for every fish they caught.

The lot of the commercial fisherman has improved little since those days. One of the great modern myths—right up there with

Welfare Mamas and Richard Gere's gerbil—is that fishermen are wealthy, if not downright filthy rich. They might be filthy, but it's from fish guts and sweat and not from a long day counting money. British Columbia, for example, has traditionally had the highest dollar-per-fish yield: until recently, the Atlantic fishery accounted for 80 percent of Canada's total catch by weight, but only 60 percent of its landed value; British Columbia returns about 15 percent of the volume, but claims one-third of the value. Pound for pound, it's a much more lucrative fishery because certain unsavoury and unpleasant circumstances have forced British Columbia to be much more open to change.

The unsavoury circumstances were created by the government-sanctioned racism that persisted in the west coast fishery until at least the 1960s. Ottawa passed immigration laws designed to effectively limit the number of people from China, Japan and India who could enter British Columbia to work as fishermen, which meant there was only a small pool of men in the traditionally underpaid immigrant workforce. These racist policies combined with (and often driven by) the powerful fishermen's unions that sprang up all along the coast meant the average fisherman in British Columbia commanded a higher wage than his east coast counterpart.

The unpleasant circumstances were the near-total collapse of the cannery trade in the 1890s; companies had expanded too quickly and, faced with a glut of canned salmon on the market, dozens of companies failed. The result was that the industry consolidated, and it's a trend that has continued to this day. Four firms produce 65 percent of the frozen salmon, and 80 percent of canned salmon and herring roe in British Columbia. One of the bigger companies to rise out of the ashes of the collapse was BC Packers, which persists as a division of Weston Foods. BC Packers, which sells the Clover Leaf brand canned salmon, and Jimmy Pattison's

75

Canadian Fishing Company, which markets Gold Seal, account for one-third of the salmon production in British Columbia. This concentration of capital, mixed with the high cost of doing business, gave British Columbia's fish companies both the incentive and the financial backing to modernize. As well, unlike the east coast fishery that grew up before the age of railroads, west coast fishermen have congregated in larger urban centres like Vancouver, Prince Rupert and Nanaimo. Because these cities provide more job opportunities when the fishing is down—and because in even the smallest community, there's always logging to fall back on—the people of British Columbia have never relied on fishing the way they do on the east coast.

Yet even in this relatively temperate business climate, one out of every four B.C. fish boats loses money, and less than half of the six thousand fishermen in this province make any more than $10,000. In fact, almost no one makes a living from fishing in this country. The typical annual net income for Canadian fishermen sits between $5,000 and $12,000, and there isn't a commercial fisherman in the country who doesn't have at least one extra job to help pay the bills. On the east coast, many fishermen have given up hope; forty thousand are listed as unemployed, costing the federal government billions. Still, people keep at it. In 1988, there were ninety-five thousand fishermen working in Canadian marine fisheries, and probably another ten thousand working the freshwater fisheries (fishermen is the operative word, by the way, since more than 90 percent of these workers are male). Add to this the seventy-five thousand processing-plant workers, and you wind up with a significant number of Canadians working at a job where they don't make a lot of money. But they're not doing it for their health, as my mother would say, or out of a love for fish. For most of these people, the fishery industry provides their only chance to make a living, particularly on the east coast where one-quarter of the population live in communities where fishing is the only game in town.

✓

The Pacific coast fishery is one of the most diverse in the country, with fishermen harvesting more than eighty different species of marine fish and shellfish. But just as on the Atlantic side, the history of the fishery is eclipsed by a single species, the sockeye salmon. As many as one-third of all fish caught in British Columbia are salmon, and half of those are sockeye; salmon account for 60 percent of the $1 billion made each year in the fishery. The next most valued species is herring, which Japanese consumers covet for its roe; herring bring in $170 million. There's also a growing groundfish industry that harvests rockfish, Pacific cod, hake, sole; the halibut fishery to the north; and the sablefish, or black cod, fishery.

Halibut used to be the third most important fish in British Columbia, and as recently as 1970 it accounted for 24 percent of the provincial catch. Halibut are ugly, flat bottom feeders, with both eyes on the same side of their heads. They can grow to enormous lengths; six-hundred-pounders are not uncommon; and they have been known to flip small boats once landed. Many a recreational fisherman on the coast secretly carries a small gun on board on those days he goes halibut hunting, to dispatch the beast while it's still in the water. But halibut is also a great eating fish, with a thick white flesh that rivals chicken for taste and texture. Because of their popularity with consumers, halibut were the first fish on the coast to suffer overfishing. As early as 1900, fishermen noticed that the halibut catch was falling off, and by 1915 the halibut fishery on both British Columbia's southern and northern shores was in serious trouble. It took the federal government five years to strike a Royal Commission, which, in 1922, recommended serious conservation measures; two years later, Canada and the United States finally signed a treaty that called for the joint regulation of the species. It took halibut stocks thirty-five years to recover, although in some places, like Halibut Flats just north of Ladner, the fish have never returned. In the early 1970s, the remaining halibut stocks were again in trouble for a different reason. They had a nasty habit of tangling themselves up in the nets of British Columbia's trawler fleet. Fishermen are allowed to take halibut only on a hook and line, so any of these fish that are trawl-caught must be released. But very few fish survive the trauma of being hauled from the sea bed to the surface in a hydraulically powered net, and thousands of halibut die every year in this process. They're victims of what's called "incidental catch," a bureaucratic euphemism that, like "friendly fire," hides a sanctioned system of carnage. Today, thanks to lower stocks and the extension of the two-hundred-mile fishing limit, which keeps British Columbia fishermen out of the great halibut waters off Alaska, halibut amount to 3 percent of the total catch.

As fish go, salmon are pretty unreliable. While they have dominated the British Columbia fishery since the first Europeans arrived, the salmon share of the total catch varies wildly. Since 1960, they've accounted for anywhere from 30 to 65 percent of fish caught in the Pacific. This variation has to do with the cyclical nature of salmon populations. Each two to seven years, salmon return to their home river to spawn; every salmon and its spawn-mates, on every river and stream along the coast, make up a genetically distinct stock—three thousand in all—that's uniquely sensitive to changes in the environment and human interference.

Sockeye have retained the cannery-day status as the most desirable of all the Pacific salmon, although many anglers would dispute the claim that they make the best eating. The sockeye's popularity rests on its distinctive, copper-coloured meat and high oil content, which makes the fish perfect for canning. But when it comes to eating, I prefer pink and small coho. They're lighter in colour and flavour, and don't leave an oily aftertaste. Sockeye spawn along the Pacific coast, from the Washington–Oregon border right up to Alaska, although there are some smaller stocks as far south as California. In the good old days, the numbers of sockeye in British Columbia waters were enormous; the Fraser River alone might have received as many as 160 million spawning sockeye in a good year. But those numbers have fallen off dramatically since the first Europeans arrived—thanks to habitat degradation and habitual overfishing, which sees 70 percent of the spawning adults destroyed each year—to the point that there are severe restrictions on sockeye catches, and the once mighty Fraser runs now average seven million fish. The decline of the sockeye lies at the heart of the British Columbia–Alaska salmon war, which dominated the headlines in August 1997. Most salmon spawned on British Columbia's rivers spend a couple of years maturing in a handy lake or pond before moving into the open ocean and heading north to Alaska. After one to three years in the ocean, they return to the river from whence they came, and this is where things get slippery. While fish in this country are generally considered finders-keepers common property, our salmon are granted a kind of honorary Canadian citizenship the moment they leave British Columbia waters. To the minds of fishermen, politicians, the DFO and even the general public, these fish are the sole property of Canada, or at least, the Canadian multinational conglomerates who control the fishery. That's all well and good, until the sockeye start the long trip back to their native waters, and they're ambushed by undiplomatic Alaskan fishermen.

The situation got so serious that in the mid-1980s—when sockeye prices were booming—the American and Canadian governments started talking about some kind of joint action, similar to the halibut treaties that had actually saved that species sixty years earlier. The problem was that, since the salmon fishery affected only British Columbia, Canada could speak with one voice, while Washington State, Oregon and particularly Alaska each had its own agenda; in fact, Washington and British Columbia had more in common than Washington and Alaska. In July of 1984, those initial talks broke down. The DFO followed with a simple act of monumental stupidity, calling on Canadian fishermen to catch as many sockeye as they possibly could in the Strait of Juan de Fuca, before they reached the U.S. boats off Point Roberts, a finger of U.S. territory ceded after the War of 1812, near the mouth of the southern arm of the Fraser. The first battle of the long salmon war had been struck, and the casualties numbered in the millions, all salmon killed by friendly fire.

Sockeye are unique for salmon in that they come in both anadromous (that is, they're born and spawn in fresh water, but spend at least part of their lives in salt water) and wholly freshwater varieties. The freshwater sockeye is called a kokanee, like the beer, and lives in many of the lakes near spawning rivers. They're a versatile fish that can, if need be, live in the sea, and that have been successfully introduced into lakes in Saskatchewan and Manitoba and into all of the Great Lakes except for Lake Ontario, for which they are eternally grateful. Kokanee are smaller than the true sockeye; the average weight is about a pound, although they've been known to reach almost ten pounds, which compares to five pounds for the sockeye to a maximum of about fifteen pounds. Like sockeye, kokanee have a dark silver back, pure white bottom, and black speckles along the sides and back. Unfortunately, kokanee share another trait with the sockeye: their numbers are in decline.

Next to sockeye, chinook are the best-known Pacific salmon species. Until recently, chinook were better known as springs, perhaps because they hatch in the spring; small springs are called "jacks" and are often designated "white" or "red" jacks, depending on the colour of their meat. Red jacks were once considered superior eating, although the difference in flesh colour is simply a genetic fluke, comparable to hair colour in humans. Commercial fishermen would throw white springs back, until, as Michael Turner tells us in his great little book *Company Town*, some marketing genius came up with this scheme: *White spring salmon. Guaranteed not to turn red in the can.* The average chinook is just over a foot long, and weighs about twelve pounds, although it is the largest of all salmon—remember the tyee?— and for that reason is prized by anglers. Chinook also migrate relatively close to shore, which leads them right into the waiting nets of the British Columbia fishing fleet, leaving many stocks overfished to the point of extinction. The Strait of Georgia, running between Vancouver Island and the mainland, offers one sad example. As recently as the 1970s, the DFO estimated the strait's chinook population to number in the hundreds of thousands. Since 1985, fishery officials have never counted more than fifteen thousand spawning chinook, and in recent years, that number has regularly dropped below five thousand. The DFO has placed severe restrictions on chinook catch quotas, although the powerful sportfishing lobby has worked overtime to keep this fish available to anglers.

Like the chinook, the coho is a popular sportfish that is also reeling from overfishing. Terry Glavin, in his book *Dead Reckoning: Confronting the Crisis in Pacific Fisheries*, cites a 1995 DFO report that stated that each year commercial and sport fishermen regularly take 70 to 85 percent of the adult coho population in the Strait of Georgia, and the coho is becoming a rare sight on a lot of the traditional spawning streams; in the spring of 1996, fishery officials on Campbell River counted only two adult coho per kilometre. These fish are prized by anglers because of their tremendous fight; they'll jump repeatedly, changing direction mid-flight, in an effort to escape the hook. While they never reach the size of the biggest chinooks, they can grow up to thirty pounds, although five to ten pounds is the norm for a fully grown adult. You can identify a coho by the grey-blue ridge along its back, its silver side and its distinctive protruding belly. The adult coho spend about eighteen months at sea before they return to the river of their birth to spawn. At this time, the fish turn crimson, with a copper-green stripe along the back, and an unmistakable hooked mouth. The natives of the west coast said that the fish were putting on their best clothes to prepare for the most important event of their lives: their marriage and subsequent death.

Pink salmon are the smallest of the Pacific salmon. Known to west coasters as "humpies," because of the large hump that grows on spawning males, the pink is now the favourite cannery salmon. The meat is light pink and not nearly as oily as sockeye, so it produces a consistent product that appeals to the salmon-salad sandwich crowd. Pink are the most abundant of all the west coast salmon, and because of their size—they average three to five pounds—and perceived adaptability, they were one of the most widely transplanted species. But efforts to introduce them to Hudson Bay, Quebec, Nova Scotia, Newfoundland, the Great Lakes, even along areas of the Pacific coast, have all ended in failure.

However, pink are thriving from Lake Ontario to Lake Superior as the result of human error. It happened in 1956, when fishery officers destined for Goose Creek, off Hudson Bay, accidentally released four hundred pink salmon into Lake Superior. The salmon were left to die, while the rest of the stock finished the journey to Goose Creek, where attempts to transplant did not succeed. Back on Lake Superior, though, a curious thing was happening. The abandoned salmon took to their new surroundings. Within two years, they spawned and the stock quickly grew.

Chum salmon are on the bottom of the list when it comes to food fish, which really has nothing to do with their taste. In fact, they're quite delicious, but their meat is a dirty white or light pink, and it's low in oil, so it was never a cannery favourite. Chum are also known as dog salmon—not to be confused with dogfish, which are a kind of small shark—because they have large, protruding teeth. In its appearance, the chum is similar to sockeye, although it grows to a much bigger size: the average chum weighs in around eleven pounds, while forty-five-pounders are common. Chum stocks are doing well compared to other salmon, but while they're not a favourite of anglers or commercial fishermen, they are an important part of the food fishery for native people along the west coast.

I pulled up to the Starbucks in Trenant Park Square, one of the newer malls on Ladner's main strip. The coffee shop was packed with Safeway and Pharmasave employees on their morning coffee break, so I grabbed a grande Mocha Frappuccino and took a seat at the last free table. Across the parking lot I could see a huge white banner with the word "Salmon" written on it in bold, red letters. Because it hung above the Superior Fish shop ("Fresh Fish

Direct From Our Boats"), I assumed it was an ad, but it could just as easily have been a gentle reminder of the way things used to be, or a herald, warning of dangers to come. The west coast fishery was in trouble. Salmon stocks had been declining for twenty years, and took a nose-dive in 1995. In the first five years of this decade, the landed value of British Columbia's commercial salmon catch averaged $211.4 million; in 1995, the value was less than half that, at $84.9 million. Along with fewer fish, the fishing fleet is besieged with problems. Changes in the unemployment insurance regulations make it harder for seasonal workers to collect the dole. Then there's a little something known as the "Mifflin Plan," which includes an $80-million government buyback of boats and licences designed to cut British Columbia's fleet of forty-three hundred boats in half by the next millennium, and—although you didn't hear this from me—hand over control of the industry in perpetuity to a select group of fish companies.

Then there was British Columbia's ever-percolating dispute with Alaska. We were six months away from the all-out war that would erupt in August. Before that battle ended, two hundred British Columbia fish boats corralled the Alaskan cruise ship *Malsapina* in Prince Rupert, near the mouth of the Skeena River. The Canadians called it a blockade to protest overfishing by Alaskan fishermen; in fact, it was a monumental display of bad manners, and a political ploy. The Americans had just walked away from talks over the Pacific Salmon Treaty, and the Canadians hoped the blockade would get them back to the bargaining table. But Canada wasn't prepared for the reaction. The U.S. Senate called on President Bill Clinton to send in the navy. Alaskan governor Tony Knowles promised legal action. In the end, the fishermen set the tourists free. They'd made their point, and while it's doubtful if their action had any real effect on the treaty process, it's certain the blockade will hurt British Columbia's $7-billion-a-year tourism industry, and particularly, the $12-million tourist trade that is the backbone of Prince Rupert's economy.

The fishermen did have a legitimate beef. The Alaskans freely admitted that they'd caught three times their quota of British Columbia–born sockeye salmon—hardly a surprise in a fishery where poaching, often under the banner of "incidental catch," runs rampant. But there may just be a hint of jealousy behind the anger; after nearly losing its wild salmon fishery, with catch levels dropping below 30 million fish in 1970, Alaska has become the best-managed and most successful fishery of its kind. Today, Alaskan fishermen are catching 220 million salmon a year, compared to the 50 million British Columbia fishermen catch—five times the fish at nearly half the cost. Meanwhile, Alaskan fishermen earn about $80,000 U.S. a year. What's really hurt British Columbia fishermen has been the glut of fish in the marketplace. Following Alaska's lead, Japan has revived its wild salmon stocks, and no longer depends on British Columbia for its supply. And in countries as diverse as Norway, Chile, and Scotland, government-sponsored fish farms have proliferated, decreasing the demand for the British Columbia product and helping to bring the price of sockeye to below seven dollars a kilogram. That's four dollars less than the fish was worth ten years ago. In one decade, British Columbia has gone from commanding 15 percent of the world's salmon market, to holding only 5 percent. And we haven't hit bottom yet.

The final act of the most recent salmon war was eerily similar to those final moments of 1984. After the breakdown of the salmon talks, and the capture of the Alaskan cruise ship, the DFO called an open season on sockeye to spite those selfish Americans, but with no thought to the actual long-term consequences of this action. It's true, the 1984 free-for-all helped bring the United States back to the bargaining table, but it virtually decimated that particular stock. It has never recovered. Will the 1997 stock suffer a similar fate?

You bet your ass it will.

The Alaskan fish war was months away, and I was content to suck back my Frappuccino and survey the Starbucks. In my tireless efforts on behalf of the Fishin' Commission to gauge the mood of the common Canadian, I struck up a conversation with the guy at the table beside me, and as luck would have it, I hit the jackpot. He introduced himself as Tim Bowling, a poet and fisherman who I'd actually worked with—although never met—ten years ago. Back then, he was editing *Flash*, an overlooked humour magazine. I'd contributed a few pieces to *Flash:* "Canada's Scarlet Men and Women," a mock history of the RCMP, and "Fishing for Canada's Soul," a kind of national identity self-assessment test. *Flash* folded years ago, and Tim now lives in Edmonton, where he's working towards his Master's degree in English and exploring his passion for poetry. A native of Ladner, he was in town to visit family and had dropped by the mall to sign copies of his first book, *Low Water Slack*; with no proper bookstore in Ladner, the Superior Fish Market was the only place selling his book.

"A lot of people find it incongruous that I'm a fisherman *and* a poet," Tim told me. "Particularly people in the literary community. Any time a poet is doing something other than teaching for a living, the writing community raises its collective eyebrows. If I was on the east coast, things might be different, because I think poetry and fishing are a much more important part of the culture there."

Tim Bowling was the antithesis of my uncle Roger; Tim was neither rough nor gnarled nor hearty, neither sunburned nor windswept; he did not wear a rubber coat, nor did he, as near as

I could tell, have a peg leg. Not once during our conversation did I hear the expression, "Arrgh, matey!" He was a well-educated, articulate young man, on the surface, indistinguishable from the shop owners, real estate agents, and urban planners who filled the coffee shop. "There's a lot of similarities between poets and fishermen," Tim said. "In both jobs, you need to develop an awareness of your environment, particularly a sensitivity to cycles and patterns. But you also have to be flexible, to deal with situations as they arise; fish, and poems, are unpredictable at the best of times."

Tim told me that he started working as a deckhand on his father Heck Bowling's fish boat the *Nola J* while he was still in high school. In 1986, after graduating from the University of British Columbia, Tim went into business with his older brother Rick, fishing in gillnetters they'd rent from the Ocean Fish Cannery in Richmond. Every summer, they would hit their favourite spots along the Fraser River, places like "Prairie Drift," "Hole-in-the-Wall" and "Canoe Pass"—names that don't appear on any map, but were familiar to anyone who has ever fished this river. "In the fifties and sixties, this was pretty much a full-time job; my father would fish eight months a year, five days a week. But the openings have been decreasing, to the point that last year the entire river was supposed to be shut down for sockeye. At the last minute, the Department of Fisheries allowed some openings. In all, the river was only open for a total of three days, but in that time, I made as much as my father would make in an entire year."

Tim and Rick concentrated their efforts on salmon, particularly the lucrative sockeye runs in August. On a good day, they averaged one hundred fish a set, which nets them about $1.50 a pound whole at the cannery in Richmond, or $3.00 a pound dressed off the dock. But like a lot of commercial fishermen, Tim talked in the past tense about his work, and confessed that he was not optimistic about his future. There were just too many people competing for an ever-diminishing resource, and to his mind, the Mifflin Plan was off the mark. "The government is trying to solve the problems in the fishery by getting rid of the independent operators, just like they're trying to get rid of the independent farms on the prairies. They hope to save the fish stocks by instituting a licence buyback, and forcing fishermen to buy a licence for each zone on the coast, at $50,000 per zone or whatever it is. Well, who the hell will be able to afford that? Some conglomerate? Or a bunch of dentists and doctors that have gotten together to buy a seiner? The simple fact is you'll probably catch all the fish you need to catch with a few strategically placed seine boats. But that's not a very good way to create employment, and that's not very damn good for people or communities."

Tim had a point. While the tradition of high capital concentration had led to a more modern fishery than on the east coast, it had also put the entire west coast industry in the hands of a select few. Most of the province's five hundred seiner fleet— those boats that fish with a purse seine—are owned by a handful of big companies, and a mere eight processors account for nearly all B.C.'s seafood production. Most of the available fishing licences aren't even owned by people who fish. Since the early 1980s, people have been allowed to sell their licences on the open market, and they've become a good investment for lawyers and dentists, even church groups have got into the act. Depending on the kind of fish it covers, a single Fraser River licence can bring in anywhere from $10,000 to, in the case of sablefish, $800,000 a year in rent.

"Where will all the fishermen go, when their boats and licences are gone?" I asked Tim, and he thought about the question for a long time.

Finally, he shrugged. "Who knows? Maybe they'll become poets?"

He looked at his watch, then gulped the rest of his coffee. He had to get going, he explained. He was doing a reading in the fish market in three minutes. He invited me along, but I had one more stop to make before I left town, and had to decline.

I watched Tim manoeuvre past the haphazard chairs and tables, then I double-checked my airline ticket. I had exactly one hour and ten minutes to go before my flight to Calgary left. It'd be cutting it close, but there was enough time. Vancouver International Airport was in Richmond, just on the other side of the George Massey Tunnel, and since I was going against the flow, traffic wouldn't be too bad. Suddenly, I was struck by a spasm of fear. What had I got myself into? Fishing was too big and too complicated an issue to be dealt with by my bargain-basement Royal Commission. Canada itself was too big and too complicated, and I felt certain that the vastness of the country would sink this project, taking my career and literary aspirations down with it. But no, I thought, no; I would not be defeated. Industry and perseverance were what made this country great; in the spirit of the *coureurs du bois* and the railwaymen and the fishermen of the mighty Fraser River, I would press on. Resolutely, I marched to the counter and boldly ordered one more Frappuccino, for the road.

Fishing for the Canadian Soul: How Do I Know I'm Canadian? A Baker's Dozen:

1. When I go to a party with people from another country, no one expects me to be interesting.
2. I can dress like I just woke up, and no one cares.
3. I feel no pressure to know a lot about wine.

4. Deep down inside, I feel that I have an innate ability to use snowshoes.

5. The entire world considers me polite, except my mom, who wishes I'd "just smarten up."

6. I got my sex education from farm animals and the Sears catalogue.

7. I know who St. Louis picked in the eighth round of the draft, and why it was a dumb idea.

8. Every so often, I get this overpowering urge to spawn.

9. I can go to a party and not dance to anything except "Twist and Shout," "The Bird Dance" and "Hey, Macarena."

10. When I see a bunch of kids playing street hockey, I get a yearning in the pit of my stomach, much akin to how the wolves in the Calgary Zoo feel when they dream of running free again on the tundra.

11. I get a twinge of pride whenever someone mentions that Montreal is the second-largest French-speaking city in the world.

12. I instinctively know what time it is in Toronto.

13. When you get right down to it, it doesn't matter to me if someone is communist or Jewish, Catholic or Anglican, French or English, or that their skin colour or cultural heritage is different from mine—I don't even care if they're a member of the federal Reform Party—just as long as they don't make noise after nine o'clock at night.

The *Barabas II* was in dire need of a paint job. The hull, once as white as a seagull's wing, was brown and peeling, the once blood-red bumper running bow to stern had turned as brown as the muddy Fraser. I had found her moored to a crooked dock just up river from Ladner, beyond a row of derelict net sheds and the skeleton of an abandoned cannery. I cautiously approached her, reluctant to disturb the peaceful flow of activity—the constant splash of the river, the nodding of old boats, the moments of silence between shithawks' calls—and uncertain of the reception I'd get from the boat's lone occupant. My stomach was tied in knots, and I braced myself with a shot of Maalox. I had not seen or spoken to my uncle for fifteen years, since that sultry summer day when my career as a commercial fisherman began. And ended.

Uncle Roger was never clear on how he actually came to own the *Barabas II*, which is strange because most old salts love to tell the story of how they got their boats. I know she was built before the war, and she had the telltale signs—the narrow hull, the slightly forward cabin—of Japanese design and craftsmanship. I suspect he bought it at an auction during the war, after the government rounded up all men, women and children of Japanese descent and interned them in prison camps in the interior. While many know of this disgraceful episode from our not-too-distant past, few realize the role fishing played in it. At the outbreak of the Second World War, Japanese Canadians were as a group the best-equipped and most effective fishermen on the coast. Their success helped to fuel a racially motivated backlash: the government deprived good people of their liberty and appropriated their land and possessions, all in the name of national security. One unspoken motive was to destroy their lock on the fishery. Uncle Roger, I suspect, was one of the beneficiaries of this shameful policy.

Perhaps he was haunted by guilt, and this fuelled the inexpressible rage he tried to muffle with a river of alcohol. It's hard to say. There'd been a woman once too, who disappeared as mysteriously as the boat appeared. Some say she died, others say she ran off in the middle of the night with his first mate, and he'd been searching the Fraser for the pair of them ever since. No matter what the source, it was clear that this man had systematically destroyed all his links to other humans, all his bridges and tunnels, to live as a floating island. In this way, I think he understood the river. Other men are attracted to the fishing life because it allows for a certain amount of autonomy, and although you're tied to the world of fish companies and unions, you can be your own boss, work your own hours with the ocean as your office. But Uncle Roger was different. Perhaps he imagined himself a romantic figure, like the river itself, a silent force of nature, with a world of wonders moving beneath his surface. In fact, he was a hermit with a job.

I stepped on board the *Barabas II* and announced myself. Silence. "Hello," I called. "Uncle Roger?"

You might think being on board the boat would bring back a flood of memories, but I recalled very little from my day as a fisherman. I do remember that we set out early in the morning, before the first freighters made their way up the river. We were fishing the "Prairie Drift" that morning and set our nets about two miles upriver, then cut our engines and floated with the current towards the mouth of the Fraser. After seven or eight passes, Uncle Roger's frustration grew. Coffee wasn't even ready yet, and he was already into his first bottle of Johnnie Walker.

We tried everything, every secret spot, every depth, every combination of wisdom and superstition that Roger could muster. Nothing. By high noon, the crew was ready to go home, but Roger would have none of that. We kept going, trying every trick in the book again and again. By six, Roger was almost incoherent from the anger and alcohol. He declared that we would make one more shot at the "Prairie Drift." We set the net, fairly shallow as I recall, some twenty fathoms and cut our engine for the slow ride downstream. We'd barely gone a hundred yards when the net began to drag, and I could feel the *Barabas II* actually slow down. We'd hit a vein of fish, and were mining it for all it was worth. Roger barked out orders, in single-word sentences. He directed me to run the net winch, although my total experience with it consisted of banging into it the night before and sustaining a huge, sockeye-coloured bruise on my thigh. I took my post and awaited my instructions.

As we hauled the net in, it was quickly evident that we hadn't just caught some salmon—the net was boiling with fish. Art Borders, the younger but much more experienced deckhand, whispered to me that he'd never seen anything like it. The old winch strained under the weight of the catch, and the boat began to list starboard as our captives moved as one to escape. I'd heard tales of boats capsized by their catch, tales usually couched in terms that made it clear that the captain had sacrificed good sense to greed. As the net drew closer and closer, the boat listed even more until we were forty-five degrees to the surface.

"We're losing her," Art said, his lips barely moving.

I can't say for sure what happened in the next moment. All I know is that we suddenly lurched forward and the *Barabas II* righted itself. Later, Art told me that I'd accidentally reversed the winch, releasing our entire catch and undoubtedly, in the process, saving the boat and crew. But at the time, I knew only Roger's rage expressed in the deep silences between his even deeper breaths.

As I thought of that day sixteen years ago, a ghost from the past appeared, standing almost right in front of me. It was Uncle Roger, older, leaner, more tanned, but still with his miles of stringy hair blowing in the wind and a two-day stubble on his chin.

"Roger!" I almost shouted his name. "You surprised me."

He just grunted and nodded.

"I suppose you be wanting a job?"

"No, actually, I just came . . ."

"Well, I got no work for you. No work for myself even . . ." His voice faded into a muttered, rambling condemnation of the government and unions.

We chatted for a while; Roger was unusually talkative, and actually used my proper first name on two separate occasions. He told me that he was more-or-less retired now that he was getting a partial pension, although he'd still take the *Barabas II* out for a run along the "Prairie Drift" whenever there was an opening. Right now, he was considering taking the government buyout, but while he wouldn't mind parting with his commercial fishing licence, he just couldn't bear the thought of losing his boat. "She's been a good friend," he said, patting the chipped rail. "We've been through a lot together."

I knew my time was growing short, and I offered Roger my hand. But instead of shaking it, he reached into his back pocket, and pulled out a crumpled envelope. He handed it to me.

"I wondered when you'd come and get this," he said, then with a brisk wave, he turned and disappeared into the cabin, leaving me alone on the deck, mumbling "See you."

I turned and made my way to the dock. I was halfway to the road when I opened the envelope. Inside was a cheque for exactly $57.63, along with a note that explained it was my wages, plus my share of the season's catch, prorated to exactly one day's work. The cheque was dated July 18, 1971; I can only assume he'd been carrying it around in his back pocket all this time, waiting with the kind of patience only a fisherman can muster.

Chapter 5

The River Runs Through It

The skinlike boundary betweeen air and water is what separates
the trout's world from ours. The line is thin but absolute, and the
fish's life is governed by many such immutable rules.

— Trout Streams of Alberta, Jim McLennan

Rainbow Trout

Taunting trout on Alberta's Bow River

S unday morning and Calgary was deserted. Although it was after 8:00 a.m., the downtown McDonald's was closed; not even the Early Bird Restaurant had opened its doors yet. In Calgary on a Sunday morning, the early bird does not get the worm, and most certainly does not get a cup of coffee. Just like Vancouver, the downtown core in Calgary is a commercial centre where lots of people work, but few of them actually live.

I was familiar with Calgary. I'd visited it several times in the course of doing research and publicity for other books, and in 1988 I took my foster son, Tony, to the Olympics, where, for the cost of about eighty-five dollars per allotted ticket, we perched at the very crest of the Saddledome—so high up Tony could actually touch the roof—and watched Finland beat Norway in a hockey game that was crucial to fans of both teams. In fact, when I was six years old, I'd lived in Calgary for a while after my father bought rights to a mine in the Rocky Mountains. We drove into town in July in the middle of a snowstorm and left in a hurry eight months later, never again to mention my father's mysterious mine.

Once, I knew my way around Calgary, but on this morning I drove for half an hour before I came across The Good Earth, a coffee shop open for business in one of Calgary's newest developments, the Eau Claire Market. Until recently, the area had been an overlooked prairie of parking lots marked here and there with the cairns of abandoned buildings. Years ago, this part of town was home to the families of men who worked at the sawmill and lumberyard across the lagoon on Prince's Island, which was named not after a member of the royal family or one of their corgis, but after the mill manager, Peter Prince. The workers called their little community Eau Claire—"clear water," according to

96

my Grade 10 French—after the town in Wisconsin where most of them had come from. In its heyday, the neighbourhood held homes and factories and warehouses, a baseball diamond and an open-air arena, the Buffalo Stadium. Today, there's an IMAX theatre, fashionable restaurants, an enormous YMCA, and of course the market itself, a post-modernist mall that, like a grasshopper, wears its skeleton, the painted iron posts and beams and conduits, on the outside. Prince's Island has also changed through the years. The industry is gone, and the island is now a municipal park with playgrounds, duck ponds and the River Café, home to the finest hamburger in town.

Eleven blocks south of the Eau Claire Market was the city's most visible landmark, the 627-foot-tall Calgary Tower. Unlike Toronto's old CN Tower, which seems fraught with psychosexual implications, Calgary's landmark is docile, simply an airport control tower on steroids; the architecture reveals nothing, hides nothing. Sometimes a tower is just a tower, as Dr. Freud might say. Although it was late September, and still early on a Calgary Sunday when I got to the attraction, there was a line out the door. Germans, mostly, as much recognizable by their designer jeans, Star Trek hairstyles and futuristic rucksacks as by their accents. As the line moved forward, I struck up a conversation with Gil, a middle-aged oil executive from Harrow-on-the-Hill, once a fashionable suburb of London, England, now an upscale district within the city. Gil was in town on business, he explained, and was spending his free day as only a middle-aged British executive could: taking holiday snaps for his family. To photograph the zoo, Stampede grounds and Olympic Park, Gil had turned down the chance to spend the day fly-fishing on the Bow River, which cuts through Calgary on just about as perfect a right angle as Mother Nature allows. There was a trace of remorse in Gil's voice, designed to let me know that while he was duty bound to take holiday snaps, his heart belonged to the river. I imagined him in a kilt and hip-waders, knee-deep in a stream in the Scottish Highlands, in his British equivalent of a Tilley hat, a wicker tackle box strapped to his waist, his bamboo fly rod bent to exhaustion from a salmon's fight. Nearby, proffering a skillet-sized net, stands Prince Charles quietly encouraging, "Keep the tip up, old man; keep the tip up." I didn't have the heart to tell Gil that it was exactly the Bow River and its fly-fishing that had brought me to Alberta and to the Calgary Tower that morning. I kept mum about my Royal Commission, and instead told Gil that I was a documentary film-maker from Ottawa researching a television special about revolving restaurants. Turning Stomachs, I called it. Gil smiled and nodded. His mind was in the moors.

From the observation terrace of the Calgary Tower—1,228.2 metres above sea level, according to the brochure—I could trace the Bow's passage through Calgary. The river approached from the west, to my left, and in the distance I could see the Rocky Mountains some 120 kilometres away. There, in the glaciers and snow, lay the source of the Bow. It weaves through the southwest corner of the northwest section Calgary, then into the heart where it frames the downtown core. Just to my right, the Bow merges with the Elbow, which flows from the huge Glenmore Reservoir directly south, and a few miles farther east, the Bow abruptly dips and makes a break for the city's southeast corner, before settling on a gentler southeastern flow. Halfway between Lethbridge and Medicine Hat, the Bow meets the Oldman River and becomes, through the corporate logic of earlier cartographers, the South Saskatchewan. To the naked eye, the Bow is just another river in a country swimming with them, but Gil understood what most Canadians, and many Calgarians, do not. Through a convergence of accidents, the section of the Bow River that runs through Calgary and on to Carsland Weir, fifteen miles to the east, is one of the finest trout steams in the world. What makes this part of the Bow so good is both the quantity of trout—some twenty-two hundred fish per mile of river, in peak season—and the quality. The fish are big, averaging nineteen inches, and regularly reach two feet in length. On any other river in North America, perhaps on earth, twenty-inch trout are harder to spot than a Progressive Conservative in the House of Commons cafeteria; on the Bow, they are the norm.

The genesis of the Bow River fishery plays like an industrial public relations film from the 1950s, for, if it wasn't for a series of environmentally unsound decisions and near-catastrophic human blunders, this world-class fly-fishing haven would not exist. The modern fishery was spawned in the spring of 1925, when a truck full of brown trout fingerlings—Scottish Lockleven brown trout, to be precise—destined to stock a stream in northern Alberta, crashed a few miles upstream from Canmore. Rather than watch the fry die, the truck driver released all forty-five thousand of them into Carrot Creek, a Bow tributary. Very quickly, the brown trout began to overrun native cutthroat and bull trout populations; browns are a hearty fish that can survive pollution and water temperatures that would kill other trout. They also spawn in the fall, when stream conditions are more stable, giving them an advantage over spring-spawning rivals. Pressure on native fish was increased during the 1940s when it was common fish management practice to stock streams and rivers with hatchery-bred rainbow trout. These hearty fish were easy to raise and, because of their tendency to jump when hooked, a favourite sportfish. Today, brown trout, rainbow trout and rainbow-cutthroat hybrids have taken over the Bow River; pure cutthroat and bull trout are rarely found on the river any more, although the government has imposed strict catch-and-release regulations in the hope stocks can be rebuilt.

In 1954, the heavy hand of humanity disrupted the river again. That was the year that the Alberta government completed the Bearspaw Dam, fifteen miles west of Calgary, designed to regulate winter water flow through the city. The result is that trout now enjoy a stable habitat, one that's much less susceptible to spring floods and summer droughts. The Bow was, and remains, Calgary's digestive system, filtering sewage, storm drain runoff and industrial outflow, and depositing it downstream, outside the city limits. Calgarians need a reliable water flow to keep their city regular. Over the past thirty years, Albertans have worked to clean up the Bow, and have instigated tough pollution control standards. In fact, the little industrial outflow and secondary sewage that makes its way into the river actually enhances the fishery. These human influences warm the winter waters—browns and particularly rainbows flourish in milder climates—and the processed sewage carries nutrients that fertilize aquatic plants, which in turn sustain a smorgasbord of insects and other small creatures upon which the trout gorge themselves. Like the MacLeod Trail, the city-long highway cum fast-food strip mall, the Bow offers an abundant food supply, conveniently located on a major access route. The trout grow fat and happy.

Angling in Alberta is growing, and in fact all the western provinces support healthy sportfisheries. It's hard to get an accurate picture of the economic importance of any given sportfishery; for some unknown but undoubtedly political reason, the DFO does not keep very good records about sportfishing. The last DFO report on this subject was the 1990 *Survey of Recreational Fishing in Canada*, published in 1995 and using figures compiled in 1985. The next report, for 1995, is not due out until 1998 at the earliest. In any case, the figures tell us that Canadian anglers caught some 300 million fish in 1985 with 90 percent of those fish taken from fresh water. The total count of sport fishermen numbered 5.5 million Canadians and another 900,000 foreigners, mostly American. In all they spent $4.4 billion, with more than half of this going towards things like hotels and motels, camp-sites, food, travel, boats and equipment, and licences. For the same year, Canada's commercial fishery brought in $3.4 billion. But it's not fair to compare the two industries, since statistics are collected very differently in each. The commercial fishery infor-mation is based on catch records and landed values, and does not include in the final tally the amount fishermen spend each year to run their business. The sportfishery uses much less formal methods for gathering information, things like market research surveys, phone polls and consumer questionnaires, and takes every red cent spent into account.

All the western provinces enjoy a healthy sportfishing trade, and even the totally landlocked Saskatchewan—with its requi-site one hundred thousand lakes—enjoys brisker sport business than Nova Scotia, New Brunswick and Prince Edward Island combined. Figures for 1985 show that anglers bought 184,000 fishing licences in Saskatchewan, and today, with its well-established network of fishing lodges and resorts, it's a $40-million industry there. Manitoba's fishery brings in about half that total—but it competes with a thriving commercial fishery. But the undoubted all-star of the west is Alberta. In five years alone, from 1975 to 1980, the number of anglers in Alberta increased from 280,000 to 374,000, while the total catch during that same period almost tripled. Today, fishing is a multimillion-dollar industry, and in a province better known for its oil and cattle, the fish are definitely biting.

My first stop in Calgary was Willow Park Village, a small strip mall just off the MacLeod Trail in the southeast corner of the city. Tucked between Stephanie's Kids clothing store and Purple Mountain, a children's outdoor clothing shop, was a haven for local fly-fishermen called Country Pleasures. The store carries everything an angler might need: magazines, books, wading boots, jackets and suspenders, hip-waders, flies, lures—even lessons in casting and fly-tying. Country Pleasures is owned and operated by Neil Jennings, a former lawyer who wanted a change of pace, and his partner, Jim McLennan, who'd kindly offered to give me some fly-fishing pointers before I made my assault on the Bow River trout.

Jim McLennan was born and raised in Edmonton, an area not known for its trout fishing. So how did he come to the sport? His father was an automotive equipment wholesaler, and a pretty good angler, although he wasn't much for fly-fishing. Every fall, a business associate named Leigh Perkins would come up from the United States and go fishing with Jim's dad. In 1965, Perkins bought the Orvis Company, the biggest name in fly-fishing equipment.

"Perkins gave my dad a fly-fishing rod," Jim told me as we sat in the office at the back of Country Pleasures. "But my dad wasn't very interested in the rod, so he gave it to me, and I was hooked right away."

Jim started reading up on the sport—beginning, of course, with the books of Roderick Haig-Brown. The more he got into it, the more interested he became.

"I think it was the scientific element that appealed to me as a teenager. It's a skill that relied less on innate ability than on practice and study. The whole premise is that you try to imitate something the fish is eating. Success is much less random; it depends on the fly you choose at that particular moment and the way you make that fly behave on the water."

In 1976, Jim moved to Calgary to go to university and got summer work as a guide on the Bow. In those days, only a handful of locals were aware of the river's potential. Typically, it was only after Americans—writing in magazines like *Field and Stream* and *Fishing World*—praised the Bow that Canadians began to appreciate their resource.

"In part, I think it was just a matter of being Canadian; we simply assumed that all those other places we read about in the outdoors magazines were superior to what we had. But also, this city really didn't have a history in sportfishing, while Canada has never developed a culture of fly-fishing like those in Britain and the United States. I'm not saying that there aren't hard-core fly-fishermen, it's just that there are less of them here. Still, in any given area you'll find little fly-fishing clubs or shops; there's even a club in Regina, although there's not a lot of fly-fishing around that city."

Today, Jim has an international reputation as an angler and fly-fishing teacher, and his two books, *Blue River Bow* and *Trout Streams of Alberta*, are best-sellers in the field. Despite the fact that fly-fishing has a snobby reputation in Canada—which probably has much to do with its close ties to the British upper classes—Jim believes that the sport is accessible to anyone.

"One myth is that it's an expensive sport, but that's really not the case. There's a range of equipment out there, priced for every kind of budget. There's also this myth that fly-fishing is a difficult sport to learn, which isn't true either. Sure, it's a difficult sport to master, and you may need to develop some basic skills before you can be successful as a novice, but it also provides more opportunities for development than other kinds of fishing."

It was time for my crash course, and Jim and I moved out to the parking lot in front of his store. He'd brought a rod and reel with him and immediately after we found a clear spot, he set up the rod and began to work the line as if this were an involuntary bodily function, like breathing.

Now, I'd always assumed that the fish, mistaking my artificial lure for a real fly, would jump out of the water and take the fly in midair. As usual, I was wrong. There are two basic kinds of flies: dry, which are designed to float on the surface, and wet, which are less buoyant and designed to hover a few inches below the water line. I was also surprised to find that I didn't use a weight; the line itself is much thicker and heavier than normal fishing line. Fly-fishing lines come in a range of weights graded from one, for the lightest, to fifteen for the heaviest, and weight is determined by the kind of fishing you're doing. If anglers need a lot of distance on their casts, are fishing for larger fish or need a lot of depth in fast water, they need a heavier line. It's an important decision because line weight determines rod selection.

"You're actually casting the line, not the fly," McLennan explains. "That's why, when we teach fly-fishing, we don't put a fly on. We want the student to concentrate on the line, and not have to worry about sticking a hook in their ear."

Jim began to wave the rod above his head, letting out a little more line with each forward thrust. "I recommend newcomers get as versatile an outfit as possible, with a five or six-weight line, and nine-foot rod with an adjustable-drag, single-action reel. It's nothing fancy, but it will allow you to deal with most of the situations that will come up on a broad-ranging river like the Bow."

It was my turn. I took the rod and tried to imitate Jim's movements. I hadn't held a fly rod in twenty-three years, since my afternoon on the Campbell River with Roderick Haig-Brown. I'd forgotten the feel of the rod. Salmon rods are short and thick and rigid; in the struggle of Man vs. Nature, Man wanted every possible advantage. But the fly rod was much lighter and more flexible. It responded to my slightest movement, creating an instant rhythm, and I understood immediately the meditative attraction the sport held for many anglers. After building what I hoped was a suitable momentum, I cast the line forward. It landed a couple of feet forward, several feet to the right.

"You're trying to throw the line," Jim said. "Relax your grip a little, and roll from the wrist, not the arm."

I tried again, this time keeping my arm steady and building a rhythm from my wrist. I cast, and to my surprise, the line lifted into the air and arched across the parking lot, landing fifty feet away at the exact moment a young woman emerged from Purple Mountain carrying a large shopping bag and a small baby.

"How they biting today?" she asked, and Jim laughed with a forced politeness that comes from hearing the same joke over and over and over again. But I did not respond. My mind was already on my next cast, and my next, and on and on until I reached the Bow River, where no fish would be safe.

What's in a name? Would not a fish by any other name smell as sweet?

The answer, when it comes to trout anyway, is there's apparently a lot to this name business. In fact, many of the trout caught on the Bow and hundreds of thousands of other rivers across this great land of ours are in fact not trout at all. Lake trout, bull trout, Dolly Varden and brook, or speckled, trout are in fact all members of the charr family, while cutthroat, brown and rainbow trout—along with its anadromous incarnation, steelhead—are the only ones who can rightfully claim the surname trout.

There are a lot of similarities between trout and charr, but the subtle differences, as Frederick Wooding points out in his essential *Lake, River and Sea-Run Fishes of Canada*, "have probably caused more anglers to become amateur ichthyologists, entomologists and limnologists than any other species of fish." The easiest way to tell the difference is to spot the spots; if the fish you just landed has small scales and grey, yellow, orange or red spots, and not black or dark brown, then it's a charr. To double-check, get the fish to say "Ahhh." If you see a little clump of teeth on the roof of its mouth, then you can be 100 percent certain that you are the proud owner of a bouncing baby charr. One more little tip; trout, without doubt, spawn in the spring, while charr, by far, spawn in fall.

You obviously won't find lake trout on the Bow River, but they are found throughout Alberta, particularly to the north, and in every province except Newfoundland. They are prized by anglers, especially the fly-camp crowd, because of their size. The second largest member of the salmon family, after tyee, lake trout regularly tip the scales at twenty pounds, and fifty-pounders are common. The official record stands at 102 pounds—that monster was netted in Lake Athabasca in northern Saskatchewan—although there are reports of a 120-pounder pulled out of Lake Superior in the early 1800s. Lake trout like big lakes, with deep, cold water, and a general rule of thumb is: the farther north you get, the bigger the lake trout.

Bull trout are native to the Bow River, and to every other Alberta river system. They are found only in Canada's western provinces and the northwestern United States, and bear a striking similarity to Dolly Varden, an often anadromous charr found along the Pacific coast, from northern Washington State to Alaska. Until recently, scientists and fishermen considered bulls a kind of Dolly Varden, but these days they recognize two distinct species; in general, bulls grow larger than Dolly Varden—to a maximum of thirty-five pounds, while Dolly Varden max out at about ten pounds—have a stubbier head, a larger mouth and a narrower body.

Bull trout are the apex hunters in the smaller, more remote creeks and streams of western Canada, where it's often slim pickings. So they've developed into an aggressive predator that'll jump at anything. Lillian Manley recalled—and kept a straight face—stories of old-timers who used live field mice for bait. So who knows? Maybe it's true? While their aggressive nature helped them move to the top of the food chain, it also contributed to their decline in Alberta. Anglers love the way they fight on the line, so they're one of the more prized sportfish in the province. They've also lost a lot of their wilderness habitat or had their regular spawning routes blocked by hydroelectric dams. Meanwhile, fishery workers have introduced non-native species to Alberta's waters, fish like rainbow and brown trout, which reproduce at a much greater rate than bulls (which take five to seven years to become sexually mature), with the result that the native species has been overrun. On top of everything else, fishermen have long considered both bull trout and Dolly Varden a nuisance because they eat the fry of more valuable species, like sockeye and lake trout. Bull trout have often been the target of bounties and other systematic slaughters to reduce their numbers. By the 1980s, the fish that had been at the start of the century the most abundant in the province was in very serious trouble. In 1993, the provincial government formed the Bull Trout Task Force, which brought together scientists, conservation groups and fishermen to deal with the crisis. Their action was swift and decisive: they made the bull Alberta's provincial fish—the only province to make such a designation—and made it illegal to kill them.

Brook trout are the smallest of Canada's misnamed charr, averaging about a foot in length and three or four pounds in weight, although ten-pounders are common. They're native to eastern Canada, and can still be found from Hudson Bay down as far south as the Mississippi headwaters. They were introduced to Alberta by federal parks officers in Banff in 1910, in the hope that they would attract anglers to the park. Today, they can be found throughout the prairies, although they're often overlooked by Alberta's anglers, who focus mainly on the bigger, feistier rainbow trout. Although they prefer cool, clean water, brookies are highly adaptable; some, called "coasters" or "slobs," can live in salt water for several months, and scientists have even cross-bred male brookies with female lake trout, producing a sterile hybrid called splake. These splake combine the best features of their parents: they have the fight and spirit of the brookie, and regularly reach lake trout weights. It's a curiously coloured fish, with a dark green back mottled with yellow squiggly lines, red fins on the lower body, and a sharply hooked lower jaw. The splake's wormlike markings come from the brookie side of the family, although that fish is usually brown or black with white markings, while it gets its fin colour from the lake trout, which has a clay-red body dotted with white speckles.

The most popular fish of the Bow River is also one of the most highly prized among Canada's anglers. Rainbow trout, in one form or another, are native to British Columbia, but proved such a hearty breed that they've been successfully introduced to almost every province. Almost too successfully, to some people's mind. In Alberta, for example, rainbow trout have overrun the native cut-throat. But not everybody is complaining. Jim McLennan told me that the rainbow of the Bow River are among the best stocks around. Nicknamed Bow River Bullets, these fish compare to ocean-run rainbow, called steelhead, of the west coast. "They fight harder, longer, faster and stronger than anything else around," Jim says. While most of Alberta's rivers now have rainbow, these are mostly transplanted. However, there is a small native population in the Athabasca River system, which runs eastward from the area of Jasper in the Rocky Mountains. This stock is a throwback from before the ice age, when the Athabasca was part of the Fraser River chain.

Rainbow trout get their name from the bright colouring along the side of their bodies. The top part is usually yellow-green or blue, and in the very middle, they have a bold pink racing stripe that runs the length of their body. In the bright sunlight, Lillian Manley told me, this stripe shimmers with all the colours of the rainbow. While it's known by dozens of local nicknames, there are three widely used names—rainbow, steelhead and Kamloops— that are the source of some confusion. Rainbow is the generic name for all the members of this family. Steelhead, often mistakenly called steelhead salmon, refers specifically to those rainbows on the coast born in fresh water that spend at least part of their life in the sea. Kamloops trout is the name for freshwater rainbows that inhabit the numerous lakes of British Columbia's southern interior. There is a tremendous variety in size: freshwater rainbow usually run two to four pounds, but the steelhead, which must compete with salmon for habitat and food, regularly reach twenty pounds and more. The record stands at forty-two pounds for a steelhead caught in Alaska. Frederick Wooding sings the praises of one particular stock of rainbow native to a river near Kootenay Lake, in British Columbia. Known as Gerrard trout, these fish average fifteen to twenty pounds, thanks to an unusually hearty diet—they feed on young kokanee salmon—and favourable spawning conditions in their home, the Lardeau River. It's not surprising that the Gerrard rainbow became one of the most popular stocked fish in the country, but with limited, and near disastrous, results. Few of the transplanted stocks stuck, while the native population on the Lardeau was almost wiped out in the rush for Gerrard trout eggs. By the mid-1930s, there were only about fifty rainbow left on the Lardeau. Serious conservation measures were invoked, and the stock eventually returned to form, but it's being threatened once again, as overfishing and habitat destruction have reduced the local kokanee, Gerrard trout's main food source. In fact, despite their hearty nature, rainbows are in serious trouble in a lot of regions. Hardest hit have been the steelhead along the coast. Once again, the source of the problem is the destruction of spawning grounds by logging, hydroelectric dams and pollution, combined with overfishing. Today, strict catch-and-release rules are in effect on most steelhead streams.

The cutthroat is the only true trout native to Alberta. They are also one of the hardest trout to get a handle on. There are at least fourteen subspecies of the cutthroat, and its marking and coloration vary widely throughout their range. Many anglers have a hard time telling them apart from rainbow trout, particularly on the Bow, where the two species have been interbreeding for decades. One clue is the presence of a coloured slash just below the gills, which gives the fish its name and helps amateur biologists make a positive identification. Cutthroat are native to both Alberta's Bow and Oldman river systems, and fishery workers have successfully seeded them in the Peace, Athabasca and North Saskatchewan river systems. But they remain a cold-water fish and prefer out-of-the-way streams to busier rivers. Like other trout, there is also an anadromous form of the cutthroat on the coast. These populations are in particular danger; many of the stocks have already disappeared from their traditional ranges in the States, while many more of the Canadian ones are in trouble. Conservationists urge fishermen to use barbless hooks and practise catch-and-release whenever they go after cutthroats.

The last trout on the Bow River is the brown trout, a member of the most illustrious trout species around. Brown trout are commonly called the "gentlemen" of the angling world, which is kind of weird when you think about it. Haig-Brown called them "the finest trout, from a fly-fisherman's point of view," and no less an authority than Izaak Walton—the founding father of angling literature—praised them in his seminal work, *The Compleat Angler*, written in 1653. In Canada, though, they can be something of a nuisance. They are native to Iceland, Britain and most of Europe, but were the stock fish of choice for the first eighty years of Canada's history. They're also by nature much more reluctant to take the hook than our native fish—which makes them a challenging quarry for advanced anglers—and can thrive in the kind of warm, dirty water that can kill a lesser trout. For these reasons, brown trout are found throughout the country, although today, they are stocked only in waters unsuitable for native trout. Like the cutthroat, there is no such thing as a typical brown trout stock. They come in a vast array of colours and markings, and are manifest in both the freshwater and sea-run varieties. They're on the smallish side for sportfish, averaging only a couple of pounds but are known to reach ten pounds or more, up to a record forty-pounder caught in Scotland in 1866.

The final Alberta fish on our plate is the mountain whitefish, a relative of the trout but actually a member of the whitefish subfamily. It's a smaller, narrower version of the lake whitefish and it looks quite similar, with a smaller, narrower body. The mountain whitefish's range is limited to western North America, from northern California up to the eastern edge of British Columbia and most of Alberta. Saskatchewan writer and fishing guru David "Carp" Carpenter compares them to the perch on the rest of the prairies, affectionately calling them "a small, dumb fish that are easy to catch." Mountain whitefish live in cold-water lakes and fast-running streams, and are prolific spawners that don't seem to be in trouble anywhere. While not exactly prized as a game fish, they do make good eating, and their abundance, small size and high oil content make them a smokehouse favourite. Still, most anglers aren't too sure about the mountain whitefish. Jim McLennan, in his *Trout Streams of Alberta,* calls them the "Miss Congeniality of the fish world," adding that few fly-fishers consider them worthy of serious pursuit.

It is true that these "Bonefish of the North" are a little hard to categorize. They don't have the noble fighting ability of a trout or the fierce disposition of a pike or muskie; neither are they viewed with the same repugnance as trash fish. Their appearance, too, is in-between: not as pretty as trout, not as ugly as suckers. A whitefish is always something of a disappointment to an angler who thinks he's hooked a trout. Even if it's a big one, nobody shouts, "Oh boy! It's a whitefish!" In Montana, they don't even give the benefit of the doubt, for the angling limit there is a nice, tidy one hundred whitefish a day.

While there's fine fishing within Calgary's city limits, and as far as the eye can see from the observation deck of the Calgary Tower, the best water is found at the southeastern edge of the city, on a fifty-six-kilometre stretch of river that runs from the Fish Creek boat launch, where Highway 22x crosses the Bow, to the town of Carsland. This is part of the river Jim McLennan calls the "blue ribbon Bow," and it just might be the greatest trout-fishing water in the world.

Midway along this blue-ribbon stretch is McKinnon Flats, a 345-acre park that the Alberta government created in 1984 and set aside for the benefit of anglers. It's not flat, as the name implies; in fact, McKinnon Flats was the first place I'd seen since I arrived in Calgary with a distinctive geographic personality. As we drove along a back road, just off Highway 22x, the Calgary flatlands opened up and we hit an abrupt decline to the edge of the Bow River two hundred feet below. My guide was Bud Livingstone, an old friend from Victoria and a classic example of the Canadian weekend fisherman. Growing up on southern Vancouver Island, Bud spent most of his spare time on the abundant breakwaters, wharfs, bridges, streams and tiny coves— anywhere that he could cast or drop a line. It was a cheap form of recreation that kept Bud, for the most part, out of trouble. After he graduated from high school and landed a sales job with Kraft Foods, Bud kept fishing. His first stop on the way up the corporate ladder was Vancouver, where he bought a fourteen-foot fishing boat for $600, which he sold for the same price two years later when he was transferred to Calgary. On moving, he was happy to discover his new job had an unexpected perk: a world-class trout stream minutes from his front door. Now, two years later, Bud was on the move again. Kraft had just named him Vancouver Island Area sales manager; he was going home. While most of his life was packed up in cardboard boxes and bouncing along the Trans-Canada Highway in the back of an Atlas moving van, Bud had set aside his rod and a few choice flies for one last day of fishing.

Bud and I pulled into the McKinnon Flats parking lot and found an empty space beside a brand-new, cream-coloured "Eddie Bauer Edition" Ford Explorer, another hint that the economic slump that hit Calgary in the late 1980s was over. I was surprised to find the lot less than quarter full; over the past few years, local anglers had been working hard to raise the profile of their sport and were meeting with some success. Their cause got a big boost in 1987 when a provincial government study found that sport-fishing was bringing $5.5 million to the local economy each year. That might seem paltry compared to the $100 million corralled by the Stampede each year, but it was a start. And then there were events like the Fall Flasher, a sit-down steak dinner and silent auction held each March at the Westin Hotel, with proceeds going to Trout Unlimited, an organization devoted to protecting wild fish habitats. Last year, 670 people shelled out for the $100-a-plate dinner, and the Fall Flasher grossed $228,000, making it the most successful fisheries' fundraiser in North America. But as I stood on the bank of one of the best trout streams in the world, on a warm, sunny fall afternoon, I wondered where all the people were.

Bud just shrugged. "More fish for us."

We strolled down to the bank of the river and stood beside a sign. "Attention Anglers," it read. "Bow River, Highway 22x to Carsland Weir, no bait. Trout catch and release, April 1 to May 31. Trout limit 2, June 1 to March 31. Trout over 40 cm must be released." In a field to our left, a Scout troop was on litter patrol, picking up discarded papers and bottles. I noticed some of them staring at us. "I get that all the time," Bud said, and I laughed because I thought he was pulling my leg. "No, I'm *serious*. It's because I bear an uncanny resemblance to Glen Clark." I looked at Bud carefully. It was true. He was about the same height, similar features, big moustache, a few pounds lighter and a few years younger than British Columbia's premier—but other than that, a spitting image. I guess I'd never noticed because I'd known Bud so long; in fact, if you ask me, Glen Clark looks like him. Nearby, a middle-aged man stood waist deep in the water, silently casting. A seven-year-old boy ran by, carrying a broken lure he'd found in the stones on the river bank. He called to his dad, twenty-five feet from shore, and proudly held up the treasure: it looked a little like a sardine can that had been run over by a tank, then left to rust in the rain. "Good work, son," the dad said, in mid-cast. "I wonder what else you can find?"

Bud and I walked a little farther up river. We reached a sharp bend, where an elderly woman had waded well out into the current. She leaned into the rushing water to maintain her balance, and cast almost to the other shore. As she reeled in, her rod arched, slacked, then arched again. "Don't get excited," she called to her husband, who was sitting on shore in a lawn chair, methodically peeling an orange. "I think I'm just snagged." As she twisted her rod to free the line, a guide boat rounded the corner and floated past her not fifteen feet away. It was a Mackenzie River Boat, so-called from the river in Oregon where they were first used. They're specially designed for anglers to use in rough, shallow water, and look very much like a dory, except rounder. The rowing seat is backward to other boats, so the guides can get a good view, back row, and slow down. Most of their customers cast towards the shore, where the water runs much slower; the guides have to slow their boats down to keep with the flow.

"Some people buy waders so they can walk out and fish the middle of the river," Bud said. "The rest buy boats so they can fish close to the shore. That doesn't quite make sense, does it?"

We found what Bud assured me was a "good spot" on the river, and got set up. Bud had brought a box of Tim Hortons doughnuts and a giant thermos of coffee, the bare essentials, he explained, for a day of fishing. As we hunched over his fly box, trying to make our minds up between the Orange Stimulator and the Crystal Blue-winged Olive, we heard a rustling in the tall grass directly behind us. Slowly, a large brown snout appeared. It mooed.

"Quiet," Bud requested, politely. "You'll scare the fish."

The cow took a step forward, and mooed again. Bud shrugged. He figured the cow must have wandered into the park through a break in the fence. McKinnon Flats is surrounded by rangeland, and in fact much of the Bow is bordered by ranches and farms, which is a source of problems for those who want to enhance the river as a fish habitat. Agriculture is Big Business in Alberta, with cattle alone worth $1.5 billion to the province's economy, and when farmers and fishers clash, the government habitually comes down on the side of the farmer.

Bud and I finally settled on the Orange Stimulators, an all-purpose, rather formless fly that looked like it could have been plucked from a child's woolly slipper. With Flossie watching, Bud entered the river. With only one rod between the two of us, we'd have to take turns. But I didn't mind letting Bud go first; I was content to watch and learn.

Bud wasted no time. Before he had even reached his spot in the river, he'd begun to work his rod, shooting line forward at an ever increasing length. By the time he planted his feet, he was making his first cast. His line arched through the air and landed almost without a splash six feet from the steep bank on the other side of the river. Bud reeled in and cast again. I watched his every nuance, but for the life of me I couldn't detect anything beyond a man, as the American humorist P.J. O'Rourke once put it, "standing in cold water up to his liver, throwing the world's most expensive clothesline at trees."

Suddenly, Bud's rod began to dip madly, and a second later a fish sprang from the water and flopped back down on its side. Bud's line zigzagged as the trout tried to break free from the hook. It jumped again, and by now it was twenty-five feet downstream from us. Bud pulled the rod sharply, to set the hook, and began to reel in his catch.

116

Two minutes later, he had the fish in his net, a foot-long rainbow trout. Gently, he held the fish by the head and removed the hook with a pair of pliers.

"I use a barbless hook, so it doesn't do as much damage," he explained. "I think most serious anglers practise catch-and-release these days."

With a twist of his wrist, Bud pulled the hook from the trout's cheek. He bent down and held the fish in the current for a moment, before letting it go.

He handed the rod to me. "Now it's your turn."

I held the rod for a moment, then gingerly walked into the river. It took a moment to get used to my borrowed hip-waders; I felt like I was adrift inside a giant rubber boot. My plan was to wade out fifteen feet or so, to the edge of the fast water, then cast to the other side where a sharp bend in the river formed a deep pool. I moved into the current, braced myself, and lifted my rod. It didn't take me long to figure out that casting in a parking lot with a hookless line was one thing; standing in the river trying to keep my balance and trying at the same time not to impale myself with the sharp part of an Orange Stimulator was another. I tried to remember Jim McLennan's advice—was that relax your wrist and roll from the arm, or vice versa?—and get a rhythm going. My first cast was relatively successful, and Bud said, after removing the hook from his sleeve, that my form was coming along nicely. My second cast was nearly perfect, sailing almost forty feet in a relatively straight line. Had it actually gone forward, it would have been even better.

Just as I was turning around to find where my fly had landed, my rod arched backward, then jerked out of my hands. It skirted across the water, hit the shore running, then disappeared into tall grass, preceded by the distinct sound of a cow mooing.

I ran to the shore, just in time to hear some Scout say to Bud, "Hey Mr. Premier, I think that cow's got your line."

Bud just shook his head. "It's not my line," he said, then pointed my way. "It's his."

Now I don't know if you've run through rangeland in a pair of hip-waders, trying to catch a distraught cow that's dragging $300 worth of fly-fishing tackle behind her, but it's not as easy as it sounds. After forty-five minutes, I managed to corner her in the parking lot with the help of the Scout troop. While a ten-year-old boy hand-fed the cow sweet grass and muttered some soothing words into her ear—the kid knew exactly what to say, as he later explained, because his father owned two hundred head of cattle— I worked the hook out of her bum. "I always use a barbless hook," I mumbled meekly, handing the rod back to Bud, tackle intact.

Bud stood quietly for a moment, sipping coffee from the thermos cup, deep in thought. Finally, he spoke.

"Next time," he suggested, "keep the tip up. And let the cow run a little more before you try to reel her in. Otherwise, I'd say you're doing fine."

Special Bonus Recipe:
Bud's Best Brown Trout Burgers

Ingredients

2 pounds brown trout fillets

2 tbsp Kraft Bullseye Hot Southern Cajun Barbecue Sauce

2 tbsp Kraft Creamy Cucumber with Dill Salad Dressing

1 tbsp Kraft Miracle Whip

½ cup pre-cooked Kraft Stove Top Cornbread Stuffing Mix

½ cup lumpy mashed potatoes

1 egg

¼ cup beer, from the bottle you're drinking

¼ cup finely minced chives

Seasoning: salt and freshly ground pepper, to taste

Grind the trout fillets in a meat grinder, or, for added enjoyment, mash them up with your fingers. Add all the ingredients, then mash them up with your fingers some more. Sip beer, before the next, most difficult stage. Using, once again, your fingers, form the mixture into medium-sized patties. Cook in a frying pan or on the barbecue over medium heat, no more than four minutes each side. Serve in hamburger buns, adding condiments to taste, and a slice of Kraft Cracker Barrel Aged Cheddar Cheese. Open another beer.

Chapter 6

The Saga of New Iceland

After Ragnarök, when Fenrir kills Óðinn, and the wolves Skoll and Hati eat the sun and the moon, when Yggdrasill, the world ash, is shaken, and the gods are defeated in final battle, all the universe will return to fire and sea. Out of that will arise an island on which will be situated the Great Hall of Gimli. All the best of men, of giants, of gods and the creatures of outer darkness will be gathered here.

— *The New Icelanders,* David Arnason

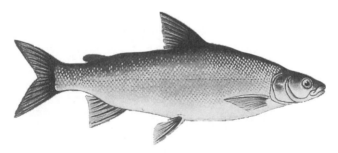

Lake Whitefish

An epic stroll through Gimli, Manitoba, whitefish capital of Canada

Sunday afternoon, and Kris' Fish and Chips was half-full. Families, mostly, who've come for pickerel cheeks, a late fall seasonal specialty in Gimli, Manitoba, and for Kris Olson's generous ice-cream sundaes. I took a table in the back, and glanced at the photocopied menu. My stomach had been killing me lately, thanks to the stress and strain of the road, and I'm not very experimental when it comes to food, particularly seafood, but I was willing to go out on a limb for the Fishin' Commission. I boldly ordered the $5.95 special and a glass of Bud, which, the waitress assured me, was the perfect drink to wash it down.

Lunch arrived a few minutes later. The plate was piled with loonie-sized pieces of fish, battered and deep-fried; pickerel cheeks, exactly as advertised. The meat was fleshier than normal fish, and a little oilier. Not bad. But then, I'd probably eat my own entrails if they were battered and deep-fried.

Outside Kris' Fish and Chips, the streets were near empty. Earlier in the year, you'd find a lot of tourists about; the annual Icelandic festival in late August, Íslendingadagurinn, alone attracts twenty thousand visitors. But now it was early October, the middle of whitefish season, and a lot of people were too busy for a Sunday stroll. I'd arrived in Gimli a couple of hours behind schedule, and missed my first meeting with David Arnason. David teaches Canadian literature at the University of Manitoba, and is a well-known poet and writer. He's also Gimli born and raised, a direct descendant of the first Icelandic settlers. Unable to get him on the phone, I set out to find him on my own. Some people outside the fish and chip shop told me they'd seen him about ten minutes earlier talking to some people near a dry dock a few blocks away. I walked south along First Avenue, past H.P. Tergesen & Sons' store, established 1899, which in its day had served double duty as a school, dance hall and theatre. Across from Tergesen's is a municipal picnic table; the sign says "No Loitering." Just down Centre Street and kitty-corner to the Country Inn Resort and Conference Centre is Gimli wharf, a living monument to the local commercial fish industry. These days, Gimli is a popular spot for tourists and retired people—townhouse complexes flourish all along the south end of the lake—and even has its share of commuters, who don't seem to mind the forty-five-mile drive into Winnipeg. But once, Gimli was best known as the most important commercial fishing town in a province with a strong, but often overlooked, fishing heritage.

We Canadians forget that Manitoba is a maritime province. It has 550 miles of coastline, which runs along the western bank of the eighth largest sea on the planet, Hudson Bay. Within its boundaries, there are more than a hundred thousand lakes, and countless rivers and streams. In fact, Manitoba is Canada's wettest province, with one-sixth of its area covered in fresh water. No wonder the province bills itself as an angler's paradise; the lakes and rivers team with trout, pike, catfish, pickerel and eighty other species. But Manitoba's strength as a sportfishery is a fairly well-kept secret, and it's the commercial fishery that's earned the province an international reputation. The Lake Winnipeg goldeye is considered one of the finest smoking fish in the world; although the fishery collapsed in the 1980s, the ancient goldeye has recently made a recovery, and these rich, rare fish claim a high price in fine restaurants from New York to Paris. Better known still is Manitoba's whitefish, which is processed on its own, or minced with northern pike, sucker (which processors cleverly market as mullet) and carp for gefilte fish, a traditional Jewish food. But a combination of overfishing and pollution, aided by the voracious sea lamprey, has all but wiped out whitefish east of the Manitoba border.

Fishing lives on in Gimli. On the government wharf, rows of heavy, narrow whitefish boats are moored, boats specially designed for the particular kind of abuse Lake Winnipeg doles out. It's a dangerous lake, 300 miles long and up to 85 miles wide, five times the size of Lake Ontario—in fact, with a surface area of 9,130 square miles, it's the third largest wholly Canadian lake—but shallow. At some points, it's barely forty feet deep. When the lake turns rough, which it can do in the wink of an eye, the waves can pummel a boat in endless succession with fifteen- or twenty-foot waves; many a boat has come down off the crest of a wave to be dashed apart on a suddenly bare lake bottom.

My quest continued. Some people told me they'd seen Arnason near the Pharmasave, but that was an hour earlier, and they doubted that even as great a talker as David Arnason would still be there. But on hearing I was writing a book about Gimli fish, they suggested I drop in on the home of Dempsey Valgardson, one of the town's most distinguished residents and a longtime fisherman. By coincidence, I knew the family. His son Bill was a well-known author, who'd taught me creative writing at the University of Victoria. I dropped in on Dempsey and Rae Valgardson just in time for a slice of homemade vínarterta, prune torte, and to talk about the old days on the lake. Dempsey is the son of one of the original Icelandic settlers, and worked for years as both a commercial fisherman and barber. Those were the days of Wynola and bootleg grain alcohol, when work was tough and money was scarce: Dempsey made twenty-five cents for a haircut, fifteen cents for a shave, and five or worse for a pound of fish. But he wasn't complaining. "I love the lake," he told me, helping himself to another piece of torte. "I always felt when I was on the lake that I was like a bird, I was free, I could go with the wind." In his day, Dempsey fought for the rights of fishermen, helping to set up the Fishermen's Federation and the Freshwater Fish

Marketing Corporation, the "Fish Pool," as the fishermen call the government agency that oversees the sale of freshwater fish caught in western Canada and parts of northern Ontario. These two organizations helped break the backs of the American combine that controlled the Lake Winnipeg fishery for decades. Now, he plays the stock market, which is maybe not so different from his days on the water.

✓

The various species of whitefish are a sub-family within the class of fish that includes salmon, trout and charr. This sub-family includes the lake whitefish, its best-known member, and its kissing cousin the mountain whitefish and ciscos, also known on Lake Winnipeg as freshwater herring. The whitefish sub-family is one of the most troubled in Canada. Not too long ago, there were seventeen separate species. But within the last twenty years, the deepwater cisco of the Great Lakes has become extinct, and conservationists have labelled three other species—the spring cisco, the kiyi and the Squanga whitefish—as vulnerable and in danger of disappearing.

Lake whitefish are found in all Canadian provinces west of the Maritimes, with a high concentration in the prairies and up north, in the Yukon and Northwest Territories. They look similar to the Atlantic salmon, although their heads and mouths are smaller, their fins sharper, and they are grey, yellow and white in colour. This fish grows to be about fifteen inches long, and reaches a weight of two to three pounds, although on the larger lakes they can easily reach fifteen or even twenty pounds and some lucky fisherman caught a forty-six-pounder in Lake Simcoe back in 1918. Whitefish prefer deeper, cooler water, and live in large schools, making them ideal for the commercial net fishery.

They're also enjoyed by local anglers, who catch them by jigging near the bottom of the lake with a baited hook. Whitefish were once the backbone of Canada's freshwater commercial fishery, although now they've almost disappeared on the Great Lakes, and have lost ground to pickerel on the prairies. Overfishing has contributed to the whitefish's decline, but a bigger problem lies in the quality of the catch. Tapeworms are commonly found in the whitefish of Manitoba and, particularly, Saskatchewan. The parasite burrows through the flesh of the fish, scarring the meat. The result is what fishermen call "cutter grade" whitefish, and although it poses little harm to humans, it's a hard sell. The fish has to be processed before it can be sold, which means a higher cost up front for a lower return. Still, the whitefish catch is the most productive one in the region covered by the Freshwater Fish Marketing Corporation—the FFMC, for short. In 1996, participating fishermen caught fourteen million pounds of whitefish, more than twice the weight of pickerel, the next highest catch. But there's been a small revival of the whitefish industry on the Great Lakes—fishermen caught eighteen million pounds there in 1996. This has helped to keep the landed value of whitefish relatively low.

After whitefish, the next most important fish on the prairies belong to the perch family. There's the misnamed pickerel—which according to Lillian Manley is not a true pickerel at all but a walleye—the sauger, and, to a lesser extent, the yellow or lake perch. Perch are one of the most distinguished fish in history. Some say that Jesus performed his miracle of the loaves and fishes with perch. They are in a sub-family of a larger group that includes sunfish, crappies and certain kinds of bass. By far the most predominant perch found in Lake Winnipeg, and throughout the prairies, are walleye. Once thought of as coarse fish, only good for fertilizer or livestock feed, by 1996, they accounted for 16 percent of the fish landings in the FFMC area and as much as 50 percent of the value. These medium-sized fish run twelve to twenty inches, and average about three pounds, although twenty-pounders are frequently found. Their name is a constant source of confusion in this country; most Canadians, and even the FFMC in its annual general report, commonly call them pickerel. But pickerel, as the name implies, are smaller members of the pike family and are relatively rare in this country. The term "walleye" is seen by many as an unruly Americanism, but there's no evidence for this; the word itself goes back to medieval English and refers to the fish's large white or opaque eye. Fishermen have several other pet names for this popular food and sportfish: yellow walleye, yellow pickerel, pikeperch, walleyed pike, walleyed perch, and, in Quebec, dory (from the French doré, or gold). The variety of nicknames reflects the wide distribution of the fish and its popularity among fishermen. Walleyes are long, narrow fish, with two fans of spiky fins on the top, two fins on each side, and one small, spiky fin on the bottom. They come in a variety of colours and markings, although they tend towards fashionable earth tones: dark greens, yellows, browns. While they are prized by anglers throughout North America for their fight and flavour, in Canada, they're the number one species anglers go after. They're also the most important stock in all of Canada's freshwater fisheries, rivalled only by the perch in landed value.

To the uninitiated, it's almost impossible to distinguish the sauger from its walleye cousins. The key is on the tail. Walleye have a white marking on the lower tip of their tail; sauger do not. They are also smaller than walleye, averaging ten to sixteen inches in length. Like the walleye, it's still a popular commercial fish in the FFMC region—almost 3 million pounds for 1996, compared to 6.8 million for walleye—however, the once lucrative German market for sauger and smaller walleye fillets is being undermined by low-priced fish from eastern Europe. The sauger's range extends through the north-central part of the continent, to the south tip of James Bay, down as far south as the Mississippi River. Sauger were also an important part of the commercial fishery on the Great Lakes, particularly Lake Erie, where fishermen used to land two to six million pounds every year. But pollution and a proliferation of larger game fish, like transplanted salmon and trout, have severely limited sauger stocks.

I thanked the Valgardsons for dessert, then walked four blocks south to the famous Gimli Viking, a twenty-foot statue unveiled in 1967 by Dr. Asgeir Asgeirsson, then president of Iceland. The Viking is standing with one foot on a rock, a sounding horn in one hand, a mighty battleaxe in the other. On his head, a seagull perched. The statue honours Gimli's unique history and heritage, and celebrates its present-day status as the largest Icelandic community outside of Iceland. Many of the old-timers grew up speaking the language of their ancestral homeland. Leo Kristjanson, the driving force behind the new museum in the old schoolhouse, told me that Icelandic was spoken in the classroom and on the playground, and it was only at university in Winnipeg that English became his main language. Now, Leo is not to be confused with Ted Kristjanson, who along with his wife, Annie, runs a museum in their backyard over on Fifth Street. Ted was a fisherman who went north to work the boats seventy-two years ago, at the age of twelve. No. Leo was the one who, like four of his brothers, earned a Ph.D., and eventually served as president of the University of Saskatchewan. Everyone in town was proud of the academic success of the Kristjanson boys; Icelanders recognize the value of a good education and have a respect for the value of literature and "book learning" unparalleled in the country. Fish and books. These are the touchstones of Icelandic history and tradition. Fish and books. These are the hallmarks of the Icelandic community in Gimli.

Icelandic settlement in Gimli and the development of the commercial fishery of Lake Winnipeg are part of the same saga. The story began in Iceland in 1874. It was, according to *The Gimli Saga*—an informal history published in 1974 by the Gimli Women's Institute—one of the worst winters on record. For the first time in living memory, saltwater bays were frozen solid. The following spring was unusually mild and marred by a series of earthquakes and volcanic eruptions. Hundreds of Icelanders lost their homes and livelihoods, while thousands more feared that the final days of fire and ice, as predicted by the *Völuspá* in the ancient saga of the Elder Edda, were at hand. Soon the world would end, and only the most righteous of men and gods would be granted everlasting life in the heaven after heaven, Gimli.

On September 10, 1874, in the northern city of Akureyri, 357 Icelanders boarded a converted cattle ship called the *St. Patrick*, bound for Canada. They represented a cross-section of Icelandic society: doctors, lawyers, teachers, merchants, fishermen and tinkers, sharing the dream of a new life in the New World. After two difficult weeks, the *St. Patrick* landed in Quebec. From there the newcomers were shipped to the immigration sheds in Toronto, then 120 miles northeast, to a temporary settlement in Kinmount, Ontario. There they were stuffed into three sheds, barely fit for livestock. That winter, every child under the age of two passed away. The dreams of many of the Icelanders died with them. Forget the stories of America they'd heard at home, how the forests were fat with fowl and game, how even the puddles were thick with fish, how there was good work for any able-bodied man. Jobs in Kinmount were scarce, and paid poorly: for a day's hard labour on the railroad, a man would bring home ninety cents; a full day's work as a farm hand earned ten cents. In May, forty of the wealthiest Icelanders moved to Nova Scotia after the provincial government assured them they'd find a better life there.

Still, some of the Kinmount settlers held onto the hope of establishing a united Icelandic community in Canada. Their last hope was Manitoba, where there was still good land to be had for anyone willing to work it. The Icelanders elected Sigtryggur Jónasson, Einar Jónasson and John Taylor, an elderly British missionary who was helping the settlers, to go explore opportunities in the west. But when they arrived in Winnipeg things did not look promising: a plague of locusts darkened the sky, destroying every crop in its path. The scouts wrote off the Red River Valley, and moved north to the Interlake region, the area bordered by Lake Winnipeg to the east and Lakes Manitoba and Winnipegosis to the west, where they found much brighter prospects. Not only was there lots of good farmland and plenty of timber, but Icelanders were first and foremost fishermen, and the surrounding lakes would provide them with food and work.

The scouting party sent word back to Kinmount: they'd found a home for the new colony. In late September 1875, the Icelanders sold what few possessions they had left and made their way to Sarnia, where they crammed onto the steamer *Ontario* to begin their journey west. The voyage across Lake Superior was harrowing: a fierce storm struck not long after the ship left port, and the lake pitched and tossed her like a rag doll for two and a half days. Eventually they reached Duluth, Minnesota, where they took the Northern Pacific Railway to a place called Fisher's Landing, North Dakota. Here, the Icelanders huddled into two open-air barges for the trip down the Red River. They landed in Winnipeg on October 11, where they were greeted by a throng of curious locals who quickly dispersed when they realized that these were in fact Icelanders, and not Eskimos as rumoured.

The journey continued.

The railroad north to Selkirk was not yet completed, so the Icelanders bought several flatboats for the voyage into Lake Winnipeg. These boats were little more than floating wooden boxes, used by locals for transporting lumber and fuel; if a storm struck on the lake, these scows would surely sink, taking the Icelanders down too. Following the lead flatboat, which the Icelanders nicknamed *Vitfirring*—"Maniac"—they made their way to the mouth of the Red River, where they were met by the *Coleville*, the only steamer on the lake. Their intended destination was Whitemud River, forty miles up the western coast of Lake Winnipeg, but barely ten miles into the trip the wind picked up, and the *Coleville*'s captain decided it would be suicide to continue; one mile from shore, he cut the flatboats loose. The gods must have been smiling on Icelanders that day, as they drifted safely to shore at a spot now known as Willow Point, one mile south of the present site of Gimli. Three hours later, inside a slapdash tent, the settlers celebrated the birth of Jón Jóhannsson, the first native-born resident of the colony of New Iceland.

The Icelanders' trials did not end at Willow Point. Over the next few years they endured starvation, a serious religious schism, and a smallpox epidemic that decimated their numbers. The winter of 1876 was particularly harsh; across the lake from Gimli, all two hundred residents of the Sandy River settlement were found dead in their cabins, the combined effect of frostbite, starvation and smallpox. Officials burned the village to the ground; the Icelanders built it back up.

Despite the hardships, the settlers persevered and turned to the lake for support. First attempts at fishing had been unsuccessful: the nets they'd brought with them were designed for the sea, and the mesh was too wide to catch Lake Winnipeg's pickerel, whitefish and sauger. Many began to think that the gods had tricked them again; there were no fish in the lake, only danger, death and empty dreams. But in the unusually mild winter of 1877, Magnus Stefanson took a small fishing party by dog sled to the northern end of the lake. One week passed, then another. Just as the settlers had given them up for dead, the fishermen returned with two hundred whitefish each and the Icelandic fishery on Lake Winnipeg was born.

Early in the new year the determined Icelanders initiated one of the grandest political experiments in Canadian history. Since the Interlake region lay beyond Manitoba's borders at the time, in the unorganized Keewatin district of the Northwest Territories, the area lacked any municipal organization. The Icelanders, with a history of democratic government that went back almost a thousand years, asked Ottawa to create an independent state—the Republic of New Iceland—with its own constitution, laws, government and language. With the support of Governor General Lord Dufferin, the Icelanders' request was granted. Quebeckers looking for a precedent to sovereignty-association need look no further than the Interlake colony: 107 years before Canada patriated the British North America Act and entrenched the Charter of Rights and Freedoms, the Republic of New Iceland ratified its own constitution. But the Icelanders did not take their special status for granted. "We must not consider ourselves as aliens, but part of the national community in which we are placed," read an editorial in *Framfari,* the local newspaper. "We must consider that in our hands lies the honour and reputation of the Icelandic nation on this continent."

The Republic lasted twelve years, a period that also saw the Lake Winnipeg fishery move from haphazard to a commercially viable enterprise. While they'd developed more effective nets and lines, the Icelanders still faced a difficult challenge: how could they get their catch to market in Winnipeg without it spoiling? It fell to outsiders to solve the problem. In the summer of 1882, a couple of fishermen named Reid and Clarke fished the lake by sailboat, which allowed them to get their catch to the big city within hours. The next year, they added another sailboat to their operation, and over the course of the summer fishing season, delivered 127,000 pounds of fresh whitefish to Winnipeg. By 1886, the Lake Winnipeg fishing fleet included seven steamboats and sixty-five sailboats, which together harvested 2.5 million pounds, most of which was processed for export to the United States. By the end of the century, the rail links to Gimli and other fishing communities were completed, and the great Manitoba commercial fishery was firmly established.

Gimli isn't the only place in the west with a fishery connection. Commercial freshwater fishermen are found throughout Manitoba, Saskatchewan, even in Alberta and Canada's north. In fact, the whitefish fishery alone on Great Slave Lake, in the Northwest Territories, is ten times more valuable than all the freshwater commercial fisheries in British Columbia combined.

Manitoba has always been the western leader when it comes to the freshwater fishery. Lake Winnipeg ports like Gimli have led the way, but there's also a significant fishery on Lakes Manitoba and Winnipegosis, and on a number of the smaller lakes that cover one-third of Manitoba's surface in fresh water. While there was a significant food fishery among the natives before the Europeans arrived, and some trade in fish between natives and the early settlers, the first experiments with a commercial fishery didn't begin until the latter half of the nineteenth century. In 1872, five men set up a fishing station on the Dauphin River, on the west-central coast of Lake Winnipeg, but the fishermen found it hard to ship their catch, and the venture soon failed. In 1882, another group of fishermen, working out of a single sailboat on Lake Winnipeg, found greater success. Within a year, fishermen were taking 127,000 pounds of mostly whitefish out of Manitoba's waters, and by the end of the decade total landings had skyrocketed to almost four million pounds.

Typically, the Manitoba fishery expanded as new technologies were introduced. First, the railway spread through the province, providing once-remote lakes with access to Winnipeg. And in 1900, an unknown Icelandic fisherman invented a tool that changed the face of the Manitoba fishery. Called a jigger, it was a device that crept along the bottom of the ice, allowing fishermen to set their nets in winter. This added a full season to the fishery, and, because of the climate, allowed fishermen to send a much fresher product to market. In the 1920s two innovations hit the lakes. The first was the appearance of gas-powered boats, which allowed captains to get around on the lake faster, gave them more power to pull their nets, and reduced the number of men needed on a boat, which lowered operating costs. The second innovation was a move from cotton nets to nylon, which were cheaper, stronger and longer-lasting. While these advances helped make the average fisherman more competitive, they had a negative effect on the fish. As early as 1884, conservationists were concerned about the fish stocks on Lake Winnipeg, and the government introduced regulations to limit the number of nets per boat and restrict most commercial fishing to the northern basin. Still, few were really concerned with the state of the fishery. In the scheme of things, it seemed relatively unimportant. Farming was, and is, Manitoba's reason for being, so much so that, at the turn of the century, the government actually paid farmers *not* to fish, so they wouldn't get caught up in such an unproductive activity.

From the start, most of Manitoba's fish were sent to the United States—a trend that continues to this day. In fact, it's been one of the most consistent factors in the commercial fishery of the country, and may account for why this industry rarely gets its due in history books and the popular imagination. Fishing defies the Harold Innis notion of a country defined by east-west communication and transportation links that evolved along with the fur trade; the fisheries grew up side by side with trading outposts, but the links tend to run north-south. In fact, this dependence on American markets meant that the various Canadian fisheries have been locked in a fierce competition, which has probably done more to encourage overfishing than anything else. The Lake Winnipeg fishery, for example, had to go head-to-head with whitefish fisheries on Lakes Ontario and Erie, which had the advantage of being much closer to several large American cities.

This competition from other Canadian markets combined with the extra transportation costs kept the price on the dock for Manitoba fish relatively low, and gave the processing companies tremendous power over the fishermen. The buyers set up little kingdoms, arbitrarily setting prices and habitually withholding payments to fishermen for months, waiting for the most opportune time. Timing made an enormous difference in a market where the wholesale price of the fish could vary 300 percent in a single season. Because of the built-in uncertainties of the business, fishermen had little equity and couldn't go to the banks for financial support. So they turned to the buyers and processors, who were often Americans, for "grubstake money," borrowing money from the same people who would set the price of their catch. The result was a perpetual cycle of debt for the fishermen; the processing companies owned their very souls. In 1928, the fishermen tried to take a stand. They set up the Manitoba Cooperative Fisheries Ltd., which tried a collective marketing approach. But the processors were too powerful, and after all, had all the cash, so they soon broke the back of the co-operatives.

The 1940s through to the mid-1960s were glory years for the Manitoba fishery. By the end of the Second World War, fishermen were taking thirty-seven million pounds of fish from Manitoba's lakes. Back then, it was mostly whitefish, sturgeon and goldeye they were after. But the sensitive lake sturgeon was soon fished out, while the advent of fast freezing, and the growth in the United States of frozen fillets and fish sticks, pushed the once despised pickerel or walleye into second spot in the popularity polls. By the end of this period, there were a number of fishermen's collectives around the province, which had led to infighting. As a result, the government set up the McIvor Commission in 1966, to investigate the fishing industry in western Canada. The commission's main proposal was that the government set up a single fish marketing agency, modelled on the wheat board. Three years later, in May of 1969, the Freshwater Fish Marketing Corporation set up shop. The FFMC is a federal Crown corporation, with a mandate to market fish "in an orderly manner" and, through its export monopoly in the west, to improve the financial lot of the average fisherman. In practical terms, this means that they offered fishermen a guaranteed price at the start of the season, which gave the independent operator the chance to do some planning.

While Manitoba fishermen are by far the biggest contributors to the FFMC—60 percent of the corporation's fish come from this province—the marketing board's area actually includes Manitoba, Saskatchewan, Alberta, the Northwest Territories, and parts of northwestern Ontario, taking in commercial fisheries operating on more than four hundred lakes. The advent of the FFMC coincided with the decline of Manitoba's fishery. By 1970, whitefish stocks were becoming seriously depleted and in April of that year the entire fishery was shut down because scientists had discovered high levels of mercury in the fish. The source of the pollution was factories along the Saskatchewan River. The lake reopened in June 1972, but, with consumer confidence down, the industry was slow to recover. Production remained low to the end of the 1970s; fishermen left the industry en masse in favour of more stable jobs in mining and forestry. In one decade, the number of commercial fishermen in Manitoba dropped 39 percent. One good thing came out of it all; whitefish stocks recovered somewhat, and for the first time in decades, the government introduced rules designed to protect the fishery.

Fishing is one of the oldest professions in Saskatchewan. Two hundred years ago, the first fur traders often set up their trading posts near good fishing spots and supplemented their income with the sale of a fish or two. By 1885 there was a true commercial fishery near Lake Qu'Appelle; that winter, fishermen took 155,000 pounds of whitefish from the lake and sold it locally. Three years later, fishermen were shipping whitefish and lake trout to the United States. As usual, the arrival of the railroad helped broaden the market for local fish, and by the mid-1920s, frozen whitefish were being shipped by rail around the country. The fishery seemed to be rolling along, but apparently not fast enough for some people. In 1910, Ottawa put together—what else—a Royal Commission to investigate the state of the fishing industry in both Saskatchewan and Alberta. Seems these farm boys weren't catching enough fish for the feds. The final report said that the industry was woefully behind the times, and that no one really cared to fix the problems. The government was so pleased with this study that it ordered another one in 1946, and got the exact same results. We're long overdue for another one, by my calculations, and I'd be happy to offer my services for a small fee and a large retainer.

In any case, while Ottawa criticized Saskatchewan, its provincial government was implementing one of the most progressive marketing policies in the country. The Saskatchewan Fish Board went to work in 1945 and tried to get a better deal for the province's fishermen. The board built processing plants, gave loans to fishermen, guaranteed landed values at the start of the season, and generally lost money. In 1949, it was replaced by the Saskatchewan Fish Marketing Service, which helped the less productive fishery in eastern Saskatchewan and encouraged fishermen the province over to form production and marketing co-ops. In 1959, the provincial government handed the keys of the SFMS to Cooperative Fisheries Limited, a marketing board run by twelve fishermen's co-ops. And on and on until 1980, when the whole thing just collapsed in the face of national and provincial recessions and the steady erosion of the industry, which saw landings sink from fifteen million pounds in 1963 to six million pounds by the early 1980s.

Today, there are about a thousand licensed fishermen in Saskatchewan. About a third of these live down south in what could be best described as a food fishery, rather than a true commercial operation. Here, it's run mostly by farmers who fish in the winter and keep most of their catch or give it away to family and friends. Most northern fishermen are natives, who fish in lakes near their home. The FFMC provides them with a subsidy of thirty cents a pound, to help cover the high cost of shipping the fish to the clearing houses in Winnipeg. Northern fishermen can also sell a portion of their catch directly to consumers and processors, although they can't export out of the province without a special permit. The catch on these northern lakes is limited to whitefish, northern pike, walleye and lake trout.

In Saskatchewan, the various groups vying for the fishery resources have a curious relationship. Native, commercial and sport fishermen co-exist in a harmony that's not found anywhere else in the country. Part of the reason is that the province clearly set its priorities years ago, so no one's jockeying for position. It also helps that the priorities actually make sense, even today. At the top of the list are treaty natives, who rely on local food fisheries to survive. Next come other subsistence fishermen, particularly those in the north. Third on the list are residential anglers; sportfishing is a huge pastime in Saskatchewan, where there isn't much else to do except play rummy—deuces wild—and write intense novellas about the endless mystery of the prairie winter. In 1993, the government sold 170,000 sport licences, mostly to residents. The final priority is the for-profit groups like commercial fishermen and sport lodge operators. It's a very democratic system, which gives the most needy people first crack at a resource that, when you get right down to it, isn't very lucrative anyway. Once again, in 1993 the landed value of all Saskatchewan fish added up to about $3 million, with the government chipping in another $200,000 in transport subsidies. The Saskatchewan agricultural sector alone is worth about two million times that amount. By clearly and sensibly setting its priorities, the province has reduced the friction between competing groups to the point that commercial fishermen and anglers have reached an unwritten time-share agreement that leaves the lakes open to the commercial fishery in late summer, when angling is at a minimum.

The Northwest Territories is also home to a dynamic commercial fishery, with most of the activity centred on Great Slave Lake.

Native commercial fishermen started working the lake in 1945, and today it generates about the same amount of money as the Saskatchewan commercial fishery. Below the Arctic tundra, fishermen take whitefish and northern pike, which is used for dog food, while arctic charr is the choice of fishermen in the far north. There's also a growing shrimp fishery off Baffin Island.

The Northwest Territories holds 9 percent of the world's freshwater resources, so it's no surprise that this region is a choice spot for the elite anglers of the world. They come to enjoy the unspoiled wilderness, pristine lakes and rivers, and most of all, fishing for arctic charr. Lillian Manley compares these fish to coho salmon in their fight and taste, and like the coho, arctic charr have both a freshwater and anadromous personality. They look similar to a lake trout, although their body and head are narrower, and they lack the bright colouring. They tend to be blue, green or brown along the back, with a white or silver belly. It's impossible to overestimate the value of the charr to the north. They are the main food for a host of large mammals, including bears, wolves and seals. They are also the primary food source for many native people and fuel their most reliable form of transport, the dog. In fact, one study figures that the so-called "subsistence" fishery of the Arctic, of which the charr is an integral part, indirectly contributes $24 million to the economy of the north by providing a stable food base and a kind of employment for as much as 75 percent of the native population. This same scenario is repeated in other remote regions of the country, where fish form the basic currency of a largely native and almost completely overlooked economy.

These days, the FFMC is sailing in some rough waters. A lot of the younger fishermen who, in Dempsey Valgardson's words, "forget how tough it used to be," want to get rid of the corporation. These young guys think that they should be able to sell their fish wherever they want, and a lot of independent and American-based proces-sors agree with them whole-heartedly. Quite often, the FFMC gets the fishermen less than top dollar for their catch. But if history pro-vides any clue, there is strength in numbers. The forces that his-torically drove prices down—a lack of equity, particularly among fishermen, and a group of processors with infinitely more economic clout than an independent fisherman—still exist. A report by fish-eries guru Brian Tobin in 1995 called for the end of corporations. But the provinces and their fishermen complained, causing Ottawa to back down. In the end, the feds offered three slight changes, to keep people happy for the time being. First, some fishermen were now allowed to sell their top-grade fish privately within the province. Second, fishermen were free to sell lower grade fish to any market they chose. And third, the appointed board for the Fish-eries Advisory Council, the group that advised the government on its freshwater fishing policy, would be replaced by an elected group. However, these measures did not address concerns about the FFMC marketing policies for lake trout and whitefish, particularly the cor-poration's various catch reduction programs, designed to control the supply of top-grade fish, to keep their value as high as possible. Don't blink; the fight over the Freshwater Fish Marketing Corpo-ration ain't over yet.

The Viking stands with his back to Lake Winnipeg, his eyes straining, from the vantage point of his pedestal, for a glimpse of Highway 9, which runs along Gimli's western edge. The lake and its fishery are slowly drifting into history. Since the 1940s, the whitefish catch has been declining; the boats still go out, but fish-ermen are working longer hours and catching fewer fish. Now, the future rides on the highway, with its tourists and commuters.

I continued walking south about a kilometre, turning off on the dirt road that leads down to Willow Point. On the south side, the road is bordered by marshlands, good catfish country. On the northern side is a single strip of small houses and winterized cabins. Someone suggested I try here for David Arnason, because his family kept a small cottage down this way, not far from the spot where the original Icelanders landed.

David saw me coming, greeted me at the door and immediately offered me a beer. A slightly stocky man, with a grey beard and long hair, he looked more like a cheerful Viking than a university professor. There was a musical quality to his voice, a lilting cadence that I had come to recognize as the Gimli accent, as distinctive as that of Cape Breton or Newfoundland. I explained that I got his name from Mary Schendlinger, a mutual friend in Vancouver, and had come to talk about Icelanders and fishing. David invited me in, and I was immediately confronted by Lake Winnipeg, washing up on shore, only a few feet from his living-room window. There was a slight chop on the water, and in the last few minutes of sunshine, shards of light spread across the waves. "This is the best place in the world to sleep," he said. "The waves come crashing in, and in a couple minutes, your heart starts beating in time to the water, and then you're asleep."

Lake Winnipeg is a curious body of water, and not just because of its size. It seems to be subject to a set of natural laws all its own. Fishermen talk of the death wave, a mysterious current unique to the lake, which passes under the ice in wintertime, killing every fish in its path. And then there's the tide, which is subject, not to shifts in the gravitational pull of the moon, but to changes in the lake's mood. Because of its hourglass shape, a strong north wind will raise the water level at the south end four or five feet in a matter of hours.

"The ocean has a slow, deep rhythm; this lake is much more explosive. It can go from dead calm to ten-foot waves in fifteen minutes. That instability has a certain charm for Icelanders, for our ancient Norse faith revolves around accident and fate, and there's a sense that the end of the world is absolutely imminent. Of course, this fatalism is the lot of all fishing peoples. Unlike the farmer, who tends to be conservative, pinning his hopes on a predictable future, the fisherman tends to be a gambler, never certain how things will turn out."

Growing up in Gimli, David says, it was impossible to escape the influence of the lake fishery. His grandfather was a fisherman, as was his father, although he got violently sick every time out; he finally quit at age thirty-five, and never went out on the water again. Many of David's friends fished, and he remembered in elementary school how classmates would disappear for weeks, having gone up to the north basin fishing stations, and a couple of years later, how many of his friends, barely teenagers, dropped out to begin their lives as career fishermen. David had a taste of the fishing life too. He remembers the living room in winter, hung with nets under repair, and his uncle waking him at five in the morning, conscripting the boy for a day on the water. The question of pay never came up; you just did it. Everybody did. At age fourteen, he regularly worked the fish boats, but he'd spent much of his time on the water aware of a gnawing terror. I wondered why, in this day and age, anyone would choose a life that was so fraught with difficulties.

David shrugged.

"I have a young cousin who's terrified on the water," he said. "He actually went overboard once, and he was in the water in a life jacket for a couple of hours. He gave up fishing for three years, he wouldn't go out on the lake at all. Now he's back at it. He tells me there's no other job he can get, there's no other way he can support himself. You see, when it's bad it's bad, but on a good day, these guys can go home with $5,000 in their pocket."

The sky was growing darker as clouds settled in from the east. In the distance, I could see a fish boat, heading due north. Whether it was heading in from a day's work, or heading out to get an early start on the morning, we could not tell.

"There were some families, like the Olsons, who considered themselves fishing dynasties. Our family was quite different in that respect. There was enormous pressure not to become a fisherman. My parents would have considered themselves defeated if I became a fisherman. I was to be sent off to get as much education as I could. My father'd say, You work hard at school. The alternative is you'll find yourself out on the water in twenty-foot waves, never knowing if you'd live to see a new day."

In a few minutes, the fish boat was lost in the distance. David and I fell into the comfortable silence of two strangers, sharing a six pack of beer, lost in our own distances, contemplating the mysteries of life, love, the universe, and fish.

Chapter 7

Some Fish, Out of Water

If someone from another planet were examining the surface of earth to determine a landing point, I'm sure they'd be drawn to the Great Lakes. They're so weird looking, you just know it must be a key area of the earth's surface. If there's intelligent life on earth, you know it would have to be around the Great Lakes.

— *A Trip Around Lake Erie,* David McFadden

Yellow Perch

Getting in touch with my inner perch,
in Port Dover, Ontario

I t had been a long, hard winter, the kind of winter I remember from my childhood, when the snow drifts grew as high as the roof on our house and, if I played my cards right and appeased the gods of weather, school itself would be forced to close its doors. Too much snow. It was spring already, but from my room at the Radisson Admiral in Toronto's Harbourfront district, I could still see piles of dirty snow melting in the afternoon sun. In the distance, the city's best-known landmark, the-tower-formerly-known-as-CN, stood taut, ready at any moment to ravage the unsuspecting SkyDome. My wife called it the City of Anger, but to me, Toronto was the Imaginary City, where nothing is exactly as it appears to be, but everything is exactly like it seems.

Don't get me wrong. I'm not one of those Toronto-hating westerners. I love Toronto. I was born just across the lake, in Hamilton, and spent much of the first thirteen years of my life in small southern Ontario towns. In fact, my wife, Barb, and I lived in Toronto for five years, and go back there whenever we can. This was just a quick stop for my Royal Fishin' Commission. My ultimate destination was Port Dover, a classic Great Lakes fishing community on the banks of Lake Erie. I'd come to Toronto to meet up with Lillian Manley and our travel guide, poet and professor David McFadden. Not that there weren't fish to be had in the waters surrounding Toronto. There used to be a great inland fishery based in the Big Smoke, but thanks to pollution, Lake Ontario's commercial fishery had been in decline for twenty-five years. In 1986, there were three thousand registered fishermen in Ontario, catching about twenty-five thousand tons of fish. Today, that number has been reduced by half, although the catch column is close to the 1986 level.

Meanwhile, sportfishing was making a comeback; my wife's City of Anger was fast becoming the City of Angler. And what were the locals going after? Try Pacific salmon, specifically pink and coho. Once, Lake Ontario had been home to native Atlantic salmon stocks, but they fell victim to pollution and overfishing long ago. For generations, people had been trying to introduce some of the more adaptable Pacific salmon species to the lakes, but it's only been fairly recently that these efforts have met with any success. Coho were first successfully stocked on the Great Lakes in 1966, and now there is a thriving self-sustaining population. The pink salmon is another story altogether. In the late 1950s, fisheries officers tried unsuccessfully to introduce this species into Hudson Bay; however, a load of Skeena River pink fry accidentally dumped into Lake Superior survived, and their descendants have spread throughout the Great Lakes. And there they are today, displaced and accidental fish, perfect quarry for the angry anglers of the Imaginary City.

From my hotel room window I could see just beyond the Whaler's Wharf Restaurant a sign advertising "Salmon Charters." Beneath it, a brand-new fishing boat, outfitted with all the latest gear and gizmos, bobs in the brown water. For a moment, my thoughts turned to folksinger Stan Rogers, that working-class visionary from southern Ontario's industrial heartland, who transformed himself into the most famous Maritimer this country has ever seen. My connection to Rogers was both distant and intimate; in 1993 I wrote *An Unfinished Conversation*, a book about his life and music. I wish I had a great Stan Rogers fishing story to tell, but unfortunately I never met the man, and only once heard him perform in person. Well, he was in person. It was at Victoria's annual

Swiftsure Yacht festival back in the summer of 1983, only a few weeks before his death. I was passed out drunk under a bush on the front lawn of the famous Empress Hotel, and Stan was on a floating dock in the Inner Harbour singing "The Jeannie C.," a plaintive ballad of a fisherman who loses his boat and barely escapes with his life.

> Come all you lads draw near to me
> And I'll not be forsaken,
> This day I lost the Jeannie C.,
> And my whole life has been taken.
> I'll go to sea no more . . .

Once, after Stan had played this song at a community hall in the village of Dover, Nova Scotia, an old salt came up to Stan and praised his work. "I've been fishing, man and boy, for these fifty years now," the old-timer said. "You said things in that song that I could only think about." For Rogers it was the ultimate compliment.

I find it interesting that in Canada, a country, we're told, founded on the National Dream of a sea-to-sea railroad, there is no great tradition of train songs. American folk music is practically founded on the rhythm of the rails and the cry of the lonesome whistle, but in Canada, outside of inspired one-offs like Gordon Lightfoot's "Canadian Railroad Trilogy" and Stompin' Tom's "Flying CPR"—songwriters seem to have very little affinity for the rails. But fish—now that's another matter. From classics like "Squid Jiggin' Ground" and "I's the B'y" to the Maritime revival spearheaded by people like Ashley MacIsaac and the Rankin Family, music informed by the fisheries has always had an important place in Canadian pop culture. And Stan Rogers was the culmination of what you might call the Fish School of Canadian songwriting. He was the first to seriously explore the contemporary possibilities of this country's traditional Maritime music, and, in the process, became so engrossed that he himself magically transformed from a big-mouthed central Canadian kid to the perfect image of the imaginary Maritime man. The song titles tell it all: "Barrett's Privateers," "Fishes," "Free in the Harbour," "Lock-keeper," "Make and Break Harbour," "Sailor's Rest," "Your Laker's back in Town," and the heartbreaking "White Squall." In a sense, Rogers created a new musical tradition based, not on what he was told was right for this country, but on what he knew in his heart was right.

Rogers's last studio album was also his most passionate musical statement. *From Fresh Water* was recorded a few months before his death and was not released until a year after. It was a homecoming for Rogers. After years of writing mostly Maritime tunes, he turned to his own province for inspiration. All the songs are set in the Great Lakes region of Ontario, a deliberate attempt to gain mass popularity in that market. Although he was only thirty-three, his stature within folk music circles was immense, and many were mentioning him in the same breath as Bob Dylan and Woody Guthrie, but he was sick and tired of standing on the verge of success and knew that if he could break in Ontario, the rest of the country would follow suit. But before the record was even released, fate stepped in. Stan was flying to his home in Dundas, Ontario, returning from a special Canada Celebration at the famous Kerrville Festival in Texas, when a fire broke out on his plane. Within minutes, the aircraft was engulfed in flames. The plane's emergency landing in Cincinnati was the top story on every TV news show for days to follow—the dramatic footage made sure of that—and although half the people on board survived the fire, Stan Rogers was not one of them. Before we knew what had happened, we'd lost another precious natural resource.

⌣

Lillian Manley hadn't spoken to me for five minutes. She was unusually distracted. Husband Number 5, the Count, had left her only a week earlier. In fact, that's why I insisted she join us. Nothing like a little fishing to take your mind off things. On top of her marital problems, we were lost again, and the early morning twilight and heavy spring rain were not making our passage any easier. David McFadden had told us that there were two main ways to get from Hamilton, on the southwest corner of Lake Ontario, to Port Dover, on Lake Erie's north shore: Highway 4 straight south, which was the direct route, or Highway 3, the more scenic trip. We opted for the scenery, and that was a big mistake. David didn't tell us that route followed the most convoluted highway on earth, and at any given point we could be heading north, south, east or west—or turn off from a major, four-lane expressway, suddenly and without warning, onto a seemingly insignificant two-lane street. After two hours of driving around in circles, I was completely disoriented and ready to stop at a gas station for directions, or, at the very least, wake David McFadden from his sound sleep in the back seat. But Lillian Manley would have none of this. She prided herself on her navigational abilities, and considered it the ultimate disgrace to have to ask for help. She could be a stubborn ass sometimes, and I told her as much. So we sat in silence.

Finally I decided to break the ice.

"You know, it's probably not our fault."

Lillian glanced over at me.

"I mean, we are in the region of the legendary Lake Erie Quadrangle, the most sinister geometric area on the planet. I'm told it puts the Bermuda Triangle to shame."

It was true. I remembered stories of the Lake Erie Quadrangle from my boyhood days in southern Ontario. It was an area of roughly twenty-five hundred square miles, cornered by Port Dover and Port Burwell on the Canadian side of the lake, and Barcelona and Conneaut on the American side. According to *Waters of Repose* by Dave Stone and David Frew, there have been 429 shipwrecks in this area; the Bermuda Triangle, by comparison, covered some fourteen thousand square miles, and had only seen 112 ships go down. At ten, these kinds of things fascinated me, along with UFOs, Sasquatches, ghosts and sea monsters, and my heart was filled with a perverse national pride in knowing that Canada's mysterious and deadly Quadrangle was much more mysterious and deadly than its more famous Caribbean counterpart; in fact by my calculations, the Lake Erie Quadrangle was twenty-one times more mysterious and deadly, if you followed a strict, shipwrecks-per-square-mile formula.

I explained all this to Lillian.

"Whatever supernatural forces are at work here have probably conspired to take us off course," I concluded, and Lillian seemed genuinely impressed.

David McFadden was rousing in the back seat. I heard him make a funny little grunting noise, then watched in the rear-view mirror as he tentatively opened one eye, then quickly closed it again. I'd met McFadden a couple of years previously, when I was working on my biography of the brilliant, troubled poet Milton Acorn. A kind of Stan Rogers antithesis, Acorn was a Maritimer who spent the better part of his life contemplating the central Canadian consciousness. McFadden had been a young man when he first met Acorn, and the old-timer took to him as he often did with aspiring writers. In an act of youthful bravery or foolishness or both, David took the ardent Stalinist Acorn to his parents' house on Hamilton's chichi mountain brow for dinner one night. David introduced Acorn to his father, a prominent doctor, and without so much as a hello, the poet grabbed a cigar from the doctor's shirt pocket. "Ah, my favourite brand," Acorn said, and promptly lit up. That was thirty years ago. Acorn is dead and buried—not deep enough for some people—and McFadden is now a respected poet and bestselling author, whose books include *A Trip Around Lake Erie*, the true story of a mythic car journey as the poet and his family searched for meaning, identity and a nice place to eat. McFadden looked nothing like a poet or professor, but more like the kind-hearted holiday camp administrator you might find in one of those old Carry On movies. Suddenly, McFadden came to life.

"Excellent," he muttered. "We're almost there." David instructed me to take the next right. Two minutes later, we rolled across the bridge at Lynn River, past the tethered fishing tugs, remnants of what once had been the world's largest freshwater fishing fleet, past the Port Dover Fish Company Fresh Fish and Seafood Retail and the Duratug Ship Yard, into Port Dover proper. Following David's directions, we headed straight to the waterfront and parked in front of a place called Callaghan's, a fresh fish restaurant right on the beach. We got out of my rented Taurus, and David and Lillian stretched as I got the fishing gear from the trunk. We'd spent the better part of the previous day scraping together equipment so we could try our luck with the perch of Port Dover; David borrowed three rods and some tackle from a neighbour, and Lillian finally persuaded the good folks at Thor's Fishing and Hunting, in Hamilton's west end, to lend us a small power boat in exchange for a free ad in the *Angler's Monthly Annual*. As I tucked the last rod under the life vests in the back of the boat,

I looked to the east. Dawn was just breaking, turning the sky a deep crimson.

"Red sky at morn, sailors be warned," David recited, cheerfully. "Who wants breakfast? I'm buying . . ."

I have no idea who named the Great Lakes, but I know one thing for certain. It wasn't a Canadian. No. The name's too immodest for Canadians, too much like bragging. The North American International Lakes, that's more like it. Or, The Conspicuously Large Lakes. In any case, there they are, laid out like a continental digestive tract that starts at the mouth of the St. Lawrence. Commercial fishing has a long history on the Lakes. We know that natives living along the lakeshore built up quite a respectable business trade in dried fish with their landlocked neighbours. With the arrival of European settlers came a much more concerted effort to exploit the fishery. By the 1790s, there were commercial fisheries on the American side of Lakes Ontario and Erie, but nothing developed in Canada until the 1820s. Lake Ontario was home to a growing whitefish trade, as was Lake Huron, which actually remained a much more valuable fishery than Lake Erie into the twentieth century. By 1851, the census reported that there were ninety-six fishermen in the province, who caught and cured 2.3 million pounds of fish. Ten years later, there were almost a thousand fishermen on the lakes. It was a time of ludicrous bounty, when there was little thought to developing a sustainable fishery. Slaughter seemed to be on everyone's mind. Whitefish were so plentiful, farmers ploughed them into their fields for fertilizer, while spawning salmon were the easiest prey. A fisheries report from the 1860s recounted the annual frenzy as the salmon made their way up Wilmot's Creek, forty miles east of Toronto, where men killed the salmon "with clubs and pitchforks, women seined them with flannel petticoats, and settlers bought and paid for farms and built houses from the sale of salmon." By the end of the century, whitefish and trout stocks were already in trouble, while the Atlantic salmon had almost disappeared.

The rapid rise of the commercial fishery and the sudden, startling decline of the fish stocks did not go unnoticed. Early in the century, the government sought to protect wild stocks, and in 1858 Upper Canada unveiled its first Fisheries Act, which tried to develop a co-ordinated approach to fish management. Today, it seems straightforward, but in its day the legislation was more controversial than gun control and abortion rolled into one because it changed the fundamental relationship Canadians had with their fish. Before 1858, fish were considered public property, beyond the influence and intrusion of the Crown; anyone was free to fish anywhere and any time they chose. But the new rules required fishermen to lease storefront property from the government in order to run their business. Since virtually every commercial fishing operation was land-based—fishermen worked with seine nets that were operated from the shore—the new rules handed the effective control over the fishery to the government. It could, in theory, limit the number of fishermen and prevent problems of overfishing. However, the people did not take kindly to the intrusion, and took their anger out on the fisheries officers hired to police the new act. At Burlington Beach, for example, the fishermen banded together and refused to lease, or let anyone else lease, the shore rights. And on Manitoulin Island, which separates Georgian Bay from Lake Huron, fisheries superintendent Bill Gibbard was murdered while investigating reports of fishing irregularities.

Today, Lake Erie supports the most lucrative of Canada's

freshwater fisheries. The industry really took off there around the turn of the century as the population, and ready market, on both sides of the lake grew. Fishing and heavy industries were operating with virtually no controls and as the new century rolled in, overfishing and pollution had taken their toll. Cisco, commonly called lake herring, and whitefish were the catch of choice in those days while other fish like pickerel, sturgeon and pike were considered nuisances and either discarded or processed for fertilizer and fuel oil. Herring was the favourite because it was the perfect fish for transport, going for days with very little spoilage, whereas other fish could start to turn bad in a matter of hours. Fishermen on both sides of the lake aggressively pursued herring—there are reports of pound nets stretched half a mile along the bottom of Lake Erie—and by the end of the Great Depression the Great Lakes herring fishery was in great trouble. In 1920, fishermen caught twenty million pounds of herring in Lake Erie alone; ten years later, that figure had dropped to under one million pounds. To pick up the slack, fishermen turned their attention to pickerel, pike and perch, and with Prohibition, many Canadian skippers tried their hand at running "midnight herring"—gin and whiskey—down south.

While greed and pollution put pressure on lake herring and whitefish in the lakes, the final blow was dealt by a prehistoric creature that has come to be known as the Dracula of the Deep. The anadromous sea lampreys were originally found only in Lake Ontario, their western range blocked by the fury of Niagara Falls. With the completion of the Welland Canal in 1829, these eel-like creatures slowly progressed into the other Great Lakes. They were first recorded in Lake Erie in 1921, and quickly moved on to Lakes Huron and Michigan. Direct ancestors of the very first vertebrates, lampreys are one of the most bizarre animals I've ever seen. They have three eyes, two on the side of the head, and one on top beside a lone nostril, and can easily reach lengths of two and a half feet. The most notable feature is the large, circular mouth, ringed by rows of razor-sharp teeth, which the lamprey uses to latch onto an unfortunate fish. That's when the lamprey's ridged tongue goes to work, boring a hole in the fish's skin. Within a few days, the host is dead, and the lamprey swims off in search of another victim. In the course of its one-year lifespan, a single lamprey can destroy forty times its own weight in fish.

During the 1930s and 1940s, lampreys spread like a virus through the Great Lakes, wiping out entire populations of herring, whitefish, lake trout, chub and burbot. The only good thing was that lamprey preferred cold-water fish, so with less competition for food and fewer predators, warm-water fish like pickerel, perch and pike thrived. The legacy of the lamprey persisted, though, and I can remember as a kid carefully hunting for them in the creeks near the Port Dover cottage my dad rented a couple of summers in a row. We'd find them resting from the currents behind rocks and stumps, and scoop them out of the water with fine mesh nets, like the ones you get with a home aquarium kit. My older brother, Greg, the braver of us, would smash their heads with a stone, and we'd bring their bodies into the bait store to collect a fifty-cent bounty. Lamprey hunting was a dangerous business though. Once, when Greg wasn't paying attention, a lamprey bit him on the heel and latched on so tight that we had to take him to the hospital in Simcoe, where the emergency room doctor cut the still squirming creature's head off with a pair of heavy utility scissors. My brother bears a nickle-sized scar on his ankle to this day. And no. We never collected our fifty-cent bounty on that one.

Despite some good years along the way, the commercial fishery on most of the Great Lakes has never recovered. Today, a multi-billion-dollar sportfishing industry has grown as conservation groups stock the lakes with trout and salmon, but the commercial fishery brings in less than $200 million. The hardest hit are Lakes Ontario and Superior, which share less than 8 percent of the total Great Lakes commercial catch. This figure is particularly shocking considering that Superior, with a total area of 32,840 square miles, is the largest freshwater lake in the world. Lakes Huron and Michigan have fared better, with the former accounting for 20 percent of the Great Lakes catch, and the latter home to the biggest freshwater catch in the United States. Best of the Lakes, though, is Erie. It accounts for three-quarters of all the fish hauled out of the Canadian side of the Great Lakes. Erie is small and shallow by Great Lakes standards: some 250 miles long and 50 miles wide at its broadest point, only slightly larger than Ontario, the smallest lake. At its deepest point, Lake Erie reaches 210 feet; Lake Huron is the next shallowest with a deepwater mark of 750 feet, while Superior goes down more than a quarter of a mile.

Along with its shallow bottom, Lake Erie has a continuous northeast flow caused by the prevailing southwesterly winds and simple physics: Lake Superior to the west is higher than Lake Erie, while Lake Ontario, to the east, is lower. So in effect, the lake acts like a vast, slow-moving river, which helps keep it relatively clean but leads to a constantly changing environment. Nowhere is this more evident than in the commercial fishing industry, where the only certainty is uncertainty. After the disasters of the 1930s and 1940s, Lake Erie fishermen turned their nets on fish called the blue pike, although, in fact, it was the blue walleye, a distant relative of the perch. Meanwhile, herring stocks made a miraculous recovery, and it seemed like the fishery had its sea legs again. However, in the two years from 1947 to 1949, herring stocks plummeted from ten million to two million pounds, and blues began their frightening decline. By 1960, the herring were gone and the blues were officially labelled extinct. This time, there was no doubt that overfishing and pollution were the culprits.

The Lake Erie fishermen persevered, and with the help of the Department of Fisheries and Oceans, converted their boats for perch, yellow pickerel and smelt. These last fish were a testament to just how unpredictable the lake can be. Fisheries officials planted smelt in the Great Lakes in the 1950s to provide food for the native lake trout. Their intent was to build trout stocks up to their historic levels, but instead, they created a new cash crop; Scott and Crossman's authoritative *Freshwater Fishes of Canada* reports that, in 1962 alone, some sixty-eight thousand Lake Erie fishermen caught 5.3 million pounds of smelt. While there was virtually no domestic market for these small, sweet, oily fish—a close relative of the Pacific oolichan—they were a particular favourite of Japanese consumers, an irony that wasn't lost on Stan Rogers when he visited Port Dover in 1982. Rogers, a staunch nationalist and working-class romantic, was appalled that the traditional ways of the Lake Erie fishermen had been co-opted by international commercial interests. He wrote "Tiny Fish for Japan," a song about the smelt fishery that appeared on his album *From Fresh Water*. It's one of Rogers's most powerful ballads, telling the story of the rise of the smelt fleet on Lake Erie, which for Rogers signalled the beginning of the end of the Great Lakes fishery.

$\mathcal{C}$

A Musical Interlude
"Tiny Fish for Japan," by Stan Rogers

Where Patterson Creek's muddy waters run down
Past the penny arcades, by the harbour downtown,
All the old turtlebacks rust in the rain
Like they never will leave here again.

But leave there they will in the hours before dawn,
Slip out in darkness without word or song;
For a few more years they'll work while they can
To catch tiny fish for Japan.

No whitefish or trout here, we leave them alone
The inspectors raise hell if we take any home.
What kind of fisherman can't eat his catch
Or call what he's taken his own?

But the plant runs three shifts now. There's plenty of pay.
We ship seventeen tons of this garbage each day.
If we want to eat fish, then we'll open a can
And catch tiny fish for Japan.

In the Norfolk Hotel over far too much beer,
The old guys remember when the water ran clear.
No poisons with names that we can't understand
And no tiny fish for Japan.

So the days run together, each one is the same.
And it's good that the smelt have no lovelier name.
It's all just a job now, we'll work while we can,
To catch tiny fish for Japan.

✓

Today, the Lake Erie fishery is once again in turmoil. This time it's not pollution or overfishing that's causing the problems; since the 1960s fisheries officials have enforced strict quotas, while the lake is cleaner than it's been in one hundred years. And that's the problem. The lake is too clean, thanks to environmental efforts and the invasion of a harmless-looking mollusc known as the zebra mussel, and the smelt are paying a heavy price. These fish feed off tiny water insects called amphipods, who in turn dine on the phytoplankton that used to thrive in the dirty old days. But these microscopic plants were fertilized by phosphate-infused soaps and laundry detergents that used to be dumped in the lake. In these phosphate-free times, the growth of phytoplankton has been severely reduced. On top of that, zebra mussels gobble up the remaining plankton. So great in number, these filter feeders recycle the entire volume of Lake Erie in a single week. The net result is a decline in food for smelt, and a dramatic decrease in the catch.

Other fish are suffering the effects of good intentions. Perch and the so-called yellow pickerel—walleye—are falling victim to life in the food chain, as anglers on the American side of the lake stock it with big trout and salmon. Over the last three years, the Port Dover fishery has been in decline, and many of the younger fishermen are trolling for other ways of making a living. I met such a man during breakfast at Callaghan's. His name was Scott Misner, a thirty-three-year-old from one of the most prominent fishing families in town. His great-grandfather Henry founded one of the first processing plants in Dover, and the family business thrived for three generations. After the death of his father, Scott says the family got out of the fish business.

"People are still fishing on the lake, but things are tough," Scott told me. "They recently got some more quota back, so maybe the government figures there are more fish out there now. That could just be because there's an election coming up. Then again, everything goes in cycles. I imagine eventually it will all come around."

Scott started fishing when he was twenty, but unlike his father and grandfather, he admits that he was less interested in the lifestyle than he was in the paycheque.

"There used to be a lot of pride and passion in the fishing industry, and for many of us it was tied to our family history. Since the 1990s, things have changed. My father fished for forty years, but he never wanted me to go into the business. He thought that there were too many problems in the industry and didn't really see a future in it. But I'm glad I did it. It allowed me to spend a lot of time on the water with my dad and experience the passion he felt for fishing. Now that he's passed away, I really appreciate that time we had together. But after he died and the family business was sold, it just wasn't the same for me."

On the Great Lakes, the commercial catch is allocated on the basis of individual quotas attached to fishermen's licences. The provinces share ownership of the fishery through their constitutional authority over property rights, which allows them to determine who can fish, to set licence fees and to establish individual quotas. This level of provincial involvement has helped to keep the industry from becoming too concentrated in one area, since the province has rarely licensed more than fifty fishermen to work out of any one port. Meanwhile, the DFO is responsible for conservation, and therefore sets seasons, catch quotas, and size and age limits for fish. In theory, it's a sensible system, keeping the competing interests—fishermen and conservationists—at arm's length. But this arrangement has put a lot of pressure on the individual fisherman of late; the increasing need to conserve stocks, combined with the DFO's general trend towards consolidating the industry and downsizing the fishing fleet, means that there are fewer and fewer licences to go around. And the only certain thing for fishermen on Lake Erie, or any of the Great Lakes, is that things in the foreseeable future will remain uncertain.

For his part, Scott hasn't fished for three years, after his arm was crushed unloading fish at the dock. A forklift slipped forward, pinning Scott's arm under a heavy box of fish. Finally, the box fell, spilling fish all over the dock. Scott's arm blew up like a balloon. Remarkably, he hadn't broken bones, but the muscle was severely damaged. "Gangrene can set in really fast in an injury like that. I was just lucky it happened on the docks; if it had happened out on the boat, miles away from home, it would have been another story."

Since then, Scott's had four operations and continues to undergo therapy. "They say I've only got 10 percent disability now. I tried to go back on the boats, but I just couldn't do it." Now he's enrolled in a woodworking technologists program at the college out in Kitchener, and doesn't pine for his days on the water. "I've just left it all in the past, and never turned back. I guess you can never really break free from the lake. I've got a two-and-a-half-year-old son, and my wife had him out fishing on the pier the other day. That's what I want to do this summer, get him out there and catch some fish."

Scott sipped his coffee, then sighed. "It's funny. We used to eat fresh fish every day. Now when we have fish, it's like Captain Highliner or Red Lobster. It's sort of pathetic, when you think about it."

Of all the fish found on Lake Erie, the perch is by far the most important, both for serious commercial guys like Scott Misner and weekend warriors like me and David McFadden. Yellow perch, to use the correct name for the species most commonly found in Canadian waters, prefer peaceful waters: brooks and streams, shallow, reedy lakeshores, the shade of docks and pilings. They are one of the most widespread of all North American fishes. They're native to central Canada right down to Kansas City, Missouri, but fishermen have introduced them to every other region on the continent, and because they are pernicious breeders—the eggs of the perch are covered by a film that fish can't digest—they can quickly take over a small lake that was once the private domain of trout or walleye. Perch are fair to middling in size: in maturity, they range anywhere from a few inches to a foot in length, perfect for the frying pan, and rarely reach a weight of much more than four pounds. And while they're not the most fierce fish that ever hit a rod, they're great eating and easy to bone, so anglers don't mind them one bit. The perch's popularity rests on the fact that they are a schooling fish that move close to the shore in the spring to spawn, providing easy access to fishermen. The Great Lakes are by far the biggest producer of perch, and although annual catches of this fish fluctuate widely— as low as three million pounds in 1948, right up to the record catch of seventy-two million pounds in 1934—these fish have provided a stable base for Ontario's fishery.

Perch are not the only fish fondly remembered by those of us who grew up in central Canada. Three fish are particularly popular: largemouth, smallmouth and rock bass. In fact, these fish are not bass at all; they're members of the sunfish family, distant relatives of both perch and true bass like striped and white bass and, just to keep you on your toes, the white perch. It's easy to distinguish the sunfish from other kinds of fish by the spiny fin that runs the length of their backs. They're also interesting because the males of the family, sensitive New Age fish that they are, take responsibility for nest-building and child-rearing. Granted, the nest is a haphazard pile of gravel, and the children are weaned within a week. But give the guys some credit for effort.

Largemouth bass are the biggest of the group of misnamed sunfish, and while they usually run around two or three pounds, they regularly reach ten pounds, and even twenty-pounders have been recorded. They look very similar to the smallmouth except that their head and, get this, their mouth are a lot bigger, extending well below and beyond the eye. In fact, they bear a striking resemblance to that old movie actor Edward G. Robinson. The largemouth is native to the waters of southern Ontario and Quebec, and can be found in some lakes in British Columbia. It's also one of the most widely transplanted fish: fish fanciers have introduced it to as diverse a range as England, South Africa, Brazil and Hong Kong. Because its range is more limited, the largemouth is less important to the sportfishery—and tourist economy—than its small-mouthed cousin, but it's still one of the most important fish in the industry.

Like the largemouth, the smallmouth bass has an extensive range, and today anglers can find transplanted stocks around the world. Originally, the smallmouth was native to the St. Lawrence basin and the Great Lakes, and it's still a favourite fish on these waters, although it is now found virtually everywhere on the continent. It's very similar to its largemouth cousin in appearance, but has a slightly smaller, thinner body and, along with the tell-tale head and mouth, the ability to change colours to blend in with its surroundings. Even though most of us consider the smallmouth bass a sportfish—anglers regularly put it near the top of the list of favourite fish—it was once a popular commercial fish as well, to the point that, even before the turn of the century, conservationists were concerned that stocks in the Great Lakes were being fished out. Today, there is no commercial catch, and anglers face daily limits and size restrictions.

The feisty rock bass rounds out the trio of most popular members of the sunfish clan. The rock bass is the smallest of the three, rarely growing beyond three pounds, but it's aggressive and quick to strike at almost any kind of lure or bait that crosses its path. They're much rounder than their big cousins, and fairly uniform in colour—a brown to green-brown body with grey or white belly. In all, it's easy to see why these sunfish bass are perennial favourites with children. They're small, nervous, impulsive, and when the mood strikes them, full of piss and vinegar. Maybe I identified with them, and perhaps, even, their plight as they struggled on the hook to free themselves from the enormous monster who had seized control of their life. These fish have a fairly limited range, which doesn't extend much beyond central North America. Historically, rock bass have been a relatively important part of Ontario's commercial fishery.

Lake herring are not actual members of the herring family. In fact, they're close relatives of whitefish, and are more properly referred to as cisco, although in some parts of the country, like Lake Winnipeg, most people know them as tullibee. Cisco are one of the most vulnerable families in our waters. The deepwater cisco, which was once found in great abundance on Lakes Huron, Superior and Michigan—and some other lakes to the north and west—is now extinct. The shortnose cisco, which roamed all the Great Lakes, is now listed as a threatened species, as are the blackfin and shortjaw ciscos. Ciscos were the favourite fish of commercial fishermen, and the leading cash crop on the Great Lakes, because they were tremendous schooling fish; if you ran into a shoal of them, you could fill your hold in a matter of hours. These small fish, which rarely grow more than a foot long, play an important role not just in our fisheries, but as a food source for other commercially significant stocks like lake trout and whitefish. In the early part of this century, the commercial herring fishery on the Great

Lakes was simply obscene, with annual catches wavering between twenty million and fifty million pounds. Most ciscoes are smoked or, because of their fine white meat, are processed for fish fingers. In appearance, the cisco resembles a small whitefish, although it can be distinguished by its characteristic protruding lower jaw, and by the patch of teeth on its tongue. They average about half a pound to a pound and a half, although in Lake Erie, they've been known to reach as much as eight pounds. Their colour varies anywhere from light blue to green to dark blue and brown.

Smelt, particularly rainbow smelt, are another small, schooling fish that has been important to the commercial fishery of the Great Lakes. Like their cousin the oolichan, rainbow smelt are an acquired taste. Slightly larger than their west coast cousins, smelt on the Great Lakes run about seven to eight inches. They're a slender fish, usually silver in colour, although in some remote lakes they tend to be darker. Smelt are found throughout Atlantic and central Canada, and also along our northeast and west coasts. While most of us think of smelt—if we think of them at all—as a commercial fish, and one that fishermen have harvested for over a hundred years, they are actually quite popular among anglers, particularly on the east coast. They're considered good eating, and because they travel in great shoals, they are easy to catch. In fact, damn easy, since smelt are the only non-bait fish Ontario fishermen are allowed to catch with a net at night. As to their curious name, smelt have a distinctive odour—often compared to fresh-cut cucumber—so fishermen didn't just see the fish when they landed a net full of them, they smelt them too.

The last of the Great Lakes commercial fish is burbot, the only completely freshwater member of the 482 species of cod. Manley calls it the "Princess Anne of Fish," since it's the least attractive member of a family not known for its good looks. It has a large, flat head taking up one-quarter of its length, and two bulging eyes, and a distinctive barb on its chin. They are medium-sized fish, averaging about fifteen inches in length, and are widely dsitributed throughout Canada. Burbot will eat anything that wanders into their deep, cold-water habitat, and don't shy away from a challenge. Wooding, in *Lake, River & Sea-Run Fishes of Canada*, tells of a fifteen-inch burbot landed by a fisherman. When he gutted it, he found a foot-long walleye digesting in its stomach. They're also well known for their spawning orgies. They join together in groups and build themselves up into a swirling, twirling mass of ugly fish ecstasy, until they can't hold on any longer. The group releases its eggs and sperm at the same time, and as many as one million little burbot babies are conceived in the moment of joyous depravity. While burbot are an important commercial fish, don't look for them in your finer restaurants. Most of them donate their livers—a superior source of vitamins A and D—to the betterment of humanity and the cod liver oil supplement industry, while the rest of their vital and not-so-vital body parts are processed for dog food. Not so long ago, burbot were labelled a troublesome coarse fish, with little commercial value. Fishermen routinely hunted and killed it so it wouldn't compete with, or destroy, more valuable fish stocks.

By the time Manley, McFadden and I emerged from our perch breakfast at Callaghan's, the sun was well into the sky. It was slightly overcast, but David assured us—and I readily agreed— that the gentle northern breeze would soon clear up the few remaining clouds. We were ready to hit the water and try our luck with the famous Lake Erie perch. I suppose we could have gone for a more glamorous fish, walleye or trout or salmon, but I had my heart set on perch. As a kid at our rented cottage in Port Dover, I'd spent my days pursuing these little creatures, and to this day, in my childhood memory, summer and perch are inseparable. Summer is the colour of perch, black back, pale almost yellow sides, belly as white as an afternoon nap. It is the taste of perch, the taste of almost brown lake water, and the smell of mud. It is the sense of anticipation, hours lying flat on the dock, the imprint of dock slats across the stomach, the sudden strike, the tremor of the rod, the feel of bare foot across the white belly, the feel of power over the powerless perch pinned to the dock. Summer is a perch waiting for death, as a hand twists the hook out of its jaw.

I vividly remember the first time I ever fished, as I think anyone who's ever fished vividly remembers the first time. It was back in the summer of 1969, and I was ten years old. It was our first day at the cottage, and I was down by the boathouse, all by myself. My older brothers had gone out in the authentic birchbark canoe that came with the summer house, but I would have none of that. In truth, I was terrified of the water, and it was enough of a chore for me to just walk on the rickety, rust-coloured dock that circled the perimeter of the boat shed. I'd come by my fear of the water honestly; at age three, I fell into our backyard pool in Ancaster, Ontario, and almost drowned. While I don't remember how I fell or for how long I struggled to save myself, I do remember the final moments, lying on the bottom just before I passed out, feeling a deep calm, staring up into the sky and thinking how beautiful the sun seemed when you saw it from underwater.

I'd gone to the boathouse to see if I could spot my brothers, and as I gingerly made my way along the very centre of the dock, afraid to get too close to either edge and accidentally fall in, I spotted something moving below. I crouched down and peered between the slats. There I saw two medium-sized perch, sunning themselves in a thin band of daylight. I say "medium-sized" but in the eyes of a child, they were monsters, easily over six inches long and, by my estimation at the time, twenty or thirty pounds apiece. I ran to the boathouse and got my dad's old spin casting rod, which had a dry stick of worm, a remnant of some distant fishing trip, impaled on the hook. Although I'd never used the rod before, I'd seen my dad with it a hundred times. I clicked the white plastic release button at the bottom of the reel and watched the weighted line drop to the boathouse floor. I reeled in three inches, and heard the reel lock into place. Having set my line, I walked back out to the dock and crouched down again. I peered through the slats, where my perch were waiting patiently. I carefully hand-fed the line, manoeuvring it a matter of inches from the perch, then I began to jig the hook up and down. To my utter amazement, the larger of the two fish immediately lunged at my line and swallowed the hook.

My rod began to dance as the distressed perch tried to throw the hook, but with the calm concentration of a veteran angler, I reeled that fish in. There was only one problem. In my excitement, I hadn't fully thought through the mechanics of the exercise. How, for example, was I going to pull a two-inch-thick perch through a one-inch gap in the dock? At first, I tried to ease her though the slats gently, but my frustration quickly grew, and within a few moments, I had both hands on the line and I was reefing it for all I was worth. Something had to give, and it wasn't the dock. I pulled too hard one too many times, and the hook flew from the perch's mouth. It just lay there on its side for a moment, then sprang back to life and swam off. I spent the rest of two summers trying to catch another perch, but I never came closer than that moment on the dock.

I told this story to David and Lillian as we were settling into our borrowed boat, and both were noticeably disgusted with my youthful cruelty. Our plan was to head to the area local fishermen call the Inner Bay, the basin of water just west of Port Dover, protected by a twenty-mile sand spit known as Long Point, the very heart of the mysterious Lake Erie Quadrangle. No one is sure why this area of the Great Lakes has seen so many shipwrecks. Perhaps it was simply because of the huge volume of ships that, until recently, jammed this major waterway. Maybe it has something to do with the shallowness of the lake, which makes it prone to sudden storms? Then there were the blackbirders, professional wreckers, who operated in these waters during the mid-1800s. These land-pirates would lure ships into treacherous waters with fake signal fires, then loot the wreckage. My own opinion, based on a solid body of scientific knowledge, is that this part of the Great Lakes is actually a centre of intense UFO activity. In March of 1864, one of the first recorded Canadian UFO sightings took place in St. Williams, a few miles west of Port Dover, when a farmer named Ziergut Eisenhauer claimed that a "flaming chariot" landed in his pasture, making off with "two hefty manhogs." Since that time, there have been thousands of UFO sightings in this part of the country.

Manley scoffed at my theory. I was always searching for something that wasn't there, she said. Then, she tends to be cynical about these sorts of things. McFadden was non-committal.

"One never knows, I suppose," he said. "But I know one thing. If someone from another planet was examining the surface of the earth to determine a landing point, I'm sure they'd be drawn to the Great Lakes. They're so weird looking, you just know it must be a key area of the earth's surface. If there's intelligent life on earth, you know it would have to be around the Great Lakes."

By now, we'd reached our destination, a small point of land that was in fact only a kilometre off St. Williams. We quickly readied our gear, opting, at Manley's suggestion, for the old standby, worms. It's funny, but I hadn't stuck one of these wriggly little creatures on a hook since I was a kid, and now, after ten years in the writing business dealing with editors and critics, I had a lot more sympathy for them. Using a medium weight, we dropped our lines almost to the bottom of the lake, then slowly reeled in a few feet. I had barely set my reel when the rod tip shook tentatively.

"You're getting a nibble," McFadden sang.

"Hold steady," Manley instructed. "Perch like to take a little taste before they commit themselves."

I held my rod firm. The tip jiggled again. Then the rod whipped down.

"Let her—" Manley began, but I stopped her mid-sentence.

"I know, I know. Let her run."

The fish took half a dozen yards of line, then I snapped into action, and reeled in for all I was worth. I actually think I was winning the fight when I suddenly realized that the sky was darkening over. I kept working the perch, but within a minute the lake had turned ugly; the wind from the southwest had picked up and was blowing a wild chop our way.

"Arrgh," moaned David. "'Tis the damnedest thing I ever seen."

We decided the most prudent course of action was to bring in our lines as fast as possible and head directly for shore where we could wait out the impending storm. But I was greedy. I'd waited twenty-seven years to catch this perch, and I wasn't about to let a little bad weather get in my way.

"I'm going to play her out," I declared.

"You must be kidding," Manley said, but when she looked in my eyes she saw the raw determination and knew that I was not to be denied.

I let the perch run again, then slowly brought her to a halt, dragging the line with my thumb. This time as I started to reel her in, she was putting up much less of a fight. Soon, I saw her break the surface, then, with a flip of her tail, drop back down a few feet.

I let her run again, but by now she had barely any fight left. She was nearly dead with exhaustion as I began my final turns.

As she got closer, David dipped the net into the water. A high wave nearly took him into the lake, but he grabbed the side in time and stabilized himself.

"For God's sake, hurry," Lillian said. "There's a goddamn white squall blowing up."

David dipped the net again, and this time the perch flopped into it. Finally, I had my fish. I held her from the bottom, careful to avoid the spiny dorsal fin, as Manley handed me the little wooden fish club, which fishermen have ironically named "the preacher." "Say your prayers, perch," I said, lifting the club over my head. But in that instant, an enormous wave struck the side of the boat, and all three of us were thrown overboard. My little perch's prayers had been answered quickly, and she darted away with a smug little flick of her tail, as my own heart sank at the prospect of three more victims lost to the mysterious Lake Erie Quadrangle. In desperation, I tucked my head down and launched into a life-saving Australian crawl. After five minutes of pushing myself to the limit, I was making little headway. I felt I was losing my fight against the forces of nature and for one brief moment thought of giving up and ending my Royal Fishin' Commission, and my life, right there in the angry lake, when I felt someone tap me on the shoulder. David McFadden stood beside me, waist-deep in water. "You know," he said, absolutely unfazed by the day's events, "I kind of fancy breakfast again. Does anyone care to join me?"

David McFadden's Pan-Fried Perch Breakfast Burgers

Ingredients

1 skillet-sized dressed whole perch per person

¼ cup milk

2 eggs per person, plus one egg

Four drops of Tabasco sauce

1 cup Ritz cracker crumbs

1 cup combined finely chopped green and red peppers,
  and sweet onion

Fresh ground pepper

2 English muffins, per person

1 slice Kraft processed cheese, per muffin

After drying yourself off completely, combine milk, one egg and Tabasco. Wash and dry dressed perch, then dip in milk mixture and roll in crushed crackers. Cook in lightly oiled skillet, over medium heat. Turn after four minutes. Meanwhile, beat remaining eggs, and pour into another lightly oiled skillet on a medium-high heat. Add chopped peppers and onions, and add liberal amounts of fresh ground pepper. Stir this mixture with a fork frequently, then lower heat and cover with a lid. While you're waiting for your fish and eggs, lightly toast English muffins. After eight minutes, remove perch from heat and carefully strip the meat from the bones. Fold fillet once, and place on lightly buttered muffin, along with scrambled egg mixture and a slice of processed cheese. Serve hot with strong coffee and a copy of the morning's newspaper.

Chapter 8

Separate Pisces

In winter, under the ice, the lake becomes a different place, a slow motion world, prehistoric, a world of great and tiny monsters, a world that a man can only see with his fish hook.
— Lamont Dore, as quoted in Lillian Manley's *Fillet of Soul*

Northern Pike

Ice-fishing for monsters, and compliments,
near Montreal, Quebec

I t's a small country.

Riding the train from Toronto to Montreal, I found myself sitting beside Lamont Dore, an acquaintance from my days in the music business. During the late 1980s, we were members of rival rock bands, not much more than teenagers chasing the shimmering lure of music stardom. My career was short-lived. I was drummer and principal songwriter for Karma Sharks, the seminal "tundra pop" band. We burst onto the scene with "The Ballad of Oedipus Rex," a song I wrote after my girlfriend at the time, a model from East Germany, left me for an American tennis player.

> Let me tell you the story of Oedipus Rex
> And how he got a big complex
> He never liked to run and play
> He'd sit all alone in his room all day
> We all thought he was a bum
> 'Til he murdered his dad and married his mom . . .

That song got a lot of local airplay and landed us a deal with the Toronto-based subsidiary of an American record label. Our next single was released with huge media push, which included an expensive supporting video directed by a nasty man with a beret and an English accent. Called simply "Moby Dick," it was a Coles Notes revision of Herman Melville's classic tale, set in a basic blues format:

> Of all the fishing stories people like to tell
> My favourite is the one about the giant white whale
> Moby Dick, Ahab loved to hate that name
> Read the book and you'll be hooked on Moby Dick . . .

The song went nowhere fast, and soon after its release, the Karma Sharks broke up. In typical music business fashion—for all its aspirations towards art, it's first and foremost an industry—the split was acrimonious, with a band of legal sharks in a feeding frenzy over copyrights and brand names and first-born sons. Lamont's music career was much longer lived. A Quebecker, he was frontman for the Octoplus, a bilingual post-punk party band that flirted with success for five or six years. In 1993, he left the band to concentrate on songwriting and production, and wrote a book based on his experiences in the music world. *Octoplussy* was a best-seller in Quebec, which in fact meant it sold enough copies to hit the best-seller lists in English Canada as well. Books and records and movies by Québécois can do very well in their home province, unlike in the rest of Canada, where you can't be a true success without leaving home.

As it turned out, we had more than just music in common. Fish, it seems, were on both our minds. Lamont was returning from a busy week in Toronto, producing several music videos, working as a guest host on Musique Plus, MuchMusic's French-language counterpart, and appearing as a separatist panellist at a debate on nationalism sponsored by either the Canada Club or Canadian Club whiskey—Lamont was never clear. Now, he was exhausted and planned to take a few days off to go fishing.

"Being in the culture business, I think I know how a fish feels," Lamont told me, unwrapping his Via Rail ham and cheese sandwich. "It's eat or be eaten; it's life in the food chain. Especially in this country. Basically, if the great whites and hammerheads don't get you, the bottom feeders will."

Lamont walked me to my hotel from the train station, and for the first time in my life I had a taste of what it felt like to be a real celebrity. As we walked through the airport, people stopped Lamont to shake his hand or ask for his autograph. One middle-aged woman in an expensive outfit nonchalantly undid her blouse as she told Lamont how much she'd enjoyed his last record, then asked him to sign her bra. He obliged without a second thought, as if he'd done it a hundred times before. Which, come to think of it, he probably had. Lamont Dore was perfect for the role of aging rocker. Swizzle-stick legs propping up a small beer gut; narrow chest and skinny arms, topped by a huge head, simply made for TV, and a mane of Clairol blond hair. His skin was a pale, translucent white, what we call in the music business a "studio tan," and he wore wire-rimmed glasses, tinted, not because he didn't want people to recognize him—he most certainly did—but because he was nearing fifty and his eyesight was failing fast. He chain-smoked thin cigarettes from Amsterdam and broke into a coughing spasm every twenty minutes, like clockwork. He looked like, as my mother would say, death warmed over. In other words, he was the personification of the Euro rock-and-roller.

The old city had changed since I last visited. Three years earlier, I'd come with my foster son, Tony, to watch the Leafs play their very last game at the Montreal Forum. Back then, Ste. Catherine Street was wall-to-wall sex shops. I remember going into one store, a great big shop that was a kind of Kmart of sex, and at one point watched a young mother, with two children sitting in her cart playing with a giant penis-shaped candle, carefully scouring a bin of discount porno movies without a trace of self-consciousness, as if she were checking the bargain bin soup cans at the corner grocery store. The old street was evolving, and many of the sex shops had already transformed into clothing boutiques with single-word names punctuated by apostrophes.

Lamont led me to a place called Dunn's, one of his favourite lunchtime haunts, where, he explained, I could get four inches of the best smoked meat I'd ever eaten, and one tiny bowl of the worst French fries I'd ever seen. I talked with Lamont about the boutiquification of the city, and asked him what it meant. Was it a reflection of the political turmoil in Quebec? Was it some kind of expression of identity? I was hoping to get Lamont going, but he merely shrugged. "It means we got our gold cards approved, so it's time to get some better disguises." The waiter brought us a couple glasses of *cinquante* and a couple smoked meat sandwiches, although we'd yet to order anything, and Lamont took a long, luscious drag on his Dutch cigarette. Suddenly a thought struck him like a hungry muskie on a twelve-dollar lure. "I will take you ice-fishing," he almost shouted. "This is Quebec, and you can't know Quebec unless you ice-fish."

✓

Lillian Manley was sitting on the couch in the lobby of the Best Western Europa, huddled around her thermos of coffee. "You're late," she snapped, although I couldn't have been more than a couple of minutes behind schedule. Perhaps she was a tad grumpy; she'd taken the last commuter jet from Toronto, and it was delayed for two hours as the maintenance crew worked to properly de-ice the wings. But that's just one of the many inconveniences you have to put up with when you live in a Nordic climate.

The moon was still high in the sky when we hit Rue Drummond. I zipped my Ski-Doo suit and fumbled to pull my hood up with mittened hands. The air was frigid, and the north wind off Mont-Royal blew right through me. Fortunately, Lamont Dore was waiting for us in his olive-green Citroën Deux Chevaux. Strapped to the roof of the car and held in place by faith and a couple of bungee cords, was "Ice Station Zebra Mussel," the tiny clapboard structure that would serve as our ice shed. Lamont had already been to the store to load up on what he said was everything we'd need for an afternoon of ice-fishing: a forty-pounder of

Five Star rye whiskey, three cases of *cinquante*, a couple magnums of cheap red wine, which was, I believe, for dessert, two packs of Colts Mild, with the chewy, wine-flavoured plastic tips, six large bags of potato chips, assorted flavours, and a dozen or so Vachon cake treats.

It was simply good luck that I'd run into Lamont. My plan all along was to try my hand at ice-fishing, a Quebec pastime that rivalled even hockey in popularity. The province's frozen lakes and rivers seemed like the last place on earth you'd expect to find sane people fishing, and yet I knew they'd be out there, packed into their Ski-Doo suits, stuffed into their little ice sheds, huddled by their oil heaters, staring at a small hole in the ice. My friend Shawn Robins once defined ice-fishing as "the transfer of fish from one freezer to another." Unless I misunderstood it, the point of the exercise was to make yourself cold and uncomfortable, then wait patiently for the opportunity to plunge your hands into freezing water. Despite the mystery, I sensed that there was something significant about this activity, something oddly Canadian, and I had come to search for that elusive "something."

Sportfishing itself is hugely popular in Quebec. Each year, 1.5 million people sportfish in the province, second only to Ontario. To give a small indication of the impact fishing has on the culture, consider the case of the *Sentier Chasse-Pêche*, a Quebec magazine that caters to the hunting and fishing crowd. This magazine has 160,000 readers, a significant chunk of Quebec's 6.5 million citizens, which makes it one of the top sellers in the country. The magazine is so popular that each year it sponsors a travelling road show, 120 shows in 104 cities and towns across the province. In fact, the total number of anglers probably exceeds the official count. Environnement et Faune Québec is the provincial ministry responsible for issuing fishing licences, and they require only one per household; on many parts of the St. Lawrence anglers don't even need a licence. What the research has shown is that the vast majority of recreational fishermen, particularly the ice-fishers, are men. "We will go through hell and back," Lamont explained, "just to get a break from our wives." Coming from a man well into his sixth marriage, I took him at his word.

Sportfishing isn't just popular, it's also an important part of the provincial economy. In 1996, anglers spent almost $2.5 million on things like tackle and bait, and the government estimated that the industry employed some twenty thousand full-time workers. Among the most popular species are perch, walleye, trout, northern pike, muskellunge, sturgeon and Atlantic salmon. Much of the appeal of sportfishing is simply due to the love Quebeckers have for the Great Outdoors, a celebration of the frontier traditions that made the province what it is. Today, 78 percent of Quebec's population live in cities, with most concentrated into the urban centres surrounding Montreal, Quebec City and Hull.

But Dore also made a good case for fish as a kind of political expression. Quebeckers are notoriously wary of big business and big government, and on a small scale, fishing is a way of asserting personal independence. A man who can fish can feed himself; it's an important statement in a province experiencing some of the highest unemployment levels in its history.

As an example of his theory, Lamont offers the case of Quebec's great salmon rivers. Up until the 1970s, most of these rivers were privately owned by "clubs" controlled by members of the Canadian Establishment and rich Americans. Those rivers the clubs didn't own they leased from the government at discount rates. The result was that recreational fishing and hunting were enjoyed only by the rich; the rest of the province was forced indoors to play or, if they couldn't resist the temptation, to poach. But in 1978 the Lévesque government decided to change the rules. They created something called *zones d'exploitation controlée*—ZECS for short—regional, non-profit, self-financing community management groups. Today, there are more than 220 of these ZECS, which provide public access to Quebec's lakes and rivers for a daily fee. Most of the money collected goes back into the management and conservation of the recreational zones. The response to the ZECS was remarkable, and the number of anglers has been growing by leaps and bounds ever since. "We fish because we can fish," Lamont said with pride. "We fish to show that we can take care of ourselves."

Sportfishing may be on the rise in Quebec, but commercial fishing is definitely on the decline. While it was never as important a part of the Quebec economy as agriculture or manufacturing, fishing had its place, especially in small communities along the Gulf of St. Lawrence and the Gaspé Peninsula. But the already low percentage of fishermen in the province's labour force has declined dramatically over the last one hundred years or so. In 1881, 1 percent of the population made its living by fishing; fifty years later, that number was down to 0.4 percent. Today, there are fewer than five thousand commercial fishermen in all of Quebec—one thousand fewer than in Prince Edward Island—which accounts for .07 percent of the population. The 1970s were a disaster for Quebec's commercial fishery; in six years the catch volume dropped from 137,000 tons to 40,700 tons. The 1980s were almost as bad. In 1986, when processors were paying higher sums for ever-scarcer supplies of cod, the Quebec fishery broke the $100-million mark for the first time in its history. Since then, catch volumes and landed values have decreased steadily, and more than two thousand fishermen have found other work. Mining and forestry are booming in the province and provide steady jobs in areas where fishing was, until recently, one of the few career choices a young man could make. Those men who stayed on the water belong to an industry that is outdated and ill-equipped to compete with Canada's other Maritime provinces. Although the Quebec government has worked to stimulate growth in the fishery, nine out of every ten boats are inshore vessels, under forty-five feet, best suited to a localized, low-volume fishery. And Quebeckers as a whole aren't big fish eaters; the per capita consumption is much lower than that of other provinces.

Quebec's commercial fishery is divided into four distinct regions: the Gaspé, which accounts for half of the province's commercial fishery; the Madeleine Islands, which take in a third; the north shore of the Gulf of St. Lawrence; and the brackish waters of the St. Lawrence River above Quebec City, where it narrows and becomes exclusively fresh water. As well, there is a tremendous native food fishery in northern Quebec and along Hudson and James bays, which has a powerful but overlooked impact on the province's economy. Cod was the traditional catch in most of the province's maritime fisheries, but the times, as the Bank of Montreal likes to tell us, they are a-changing. Today, shellfish keep the fishery afloat; in all, lobster, snow crab and shrimp make up 70 percent of the landed value.

Lamont Dore was explaining the significance of alcohol to me and Lillian Manley.

"You can't go ice-fishing without a healthy supply of booze," he said. "It acts as a kind of antifreeze, protecting the body from extreme cold and warding off hypothermia. It also leads you towards spiritual catharsis and epiphany."

Manley looked at him and rolled her eyes. "And I thought this was just a cheap excuse to get pissed." We'd just turned onto

Boulevard René Lévesque, and were heading east towards the highway that would take us out of town. The street name, I thought, was a stroke of genius. I'm sure it's a constant source of irritation to Montreal's federalists, and therein lay its beauty. Was there a street name anywhere else in this country that could set people off like Boulevard René Lévesque? I doubt it, unless Calgary secretly has a Preston Manning Avenue in the works.

By virtue of his experience, Lamont had taken command of our team, and I sensed some resentment on Manley's part. She was a control freak and was still a little under the weather, emotionally speaking, in the aftermath of the Count's departure. From the start, Manley had made no effort to hide her contempt for ice-fishing. It was, in her words, a "stupid sport" for "louts and lazy men," and required less skill, by her estimation, than one needed to piss into a manhole. Lamont did not rise to the bait. "Seems crazy, doesn't it?" he said. "But there's just something about it I find irresistible, like the charms of a beautiful woman." He glanced at Manley and smiled a big, toothy smile that I think was supposed to be sexy.

"I've ice-fished in every province in the country," Lamont said. "It's interesting, the subtle differences you find. In Ontario, it's a business thing, a kind of frozen lunch meeting, where young men and women get together to network and close deals. On the prairies, where the winter is twice as long, it has an economic motivation; people are out to fill their freezer for the winter. In B.C.—well, I'm not so sure. I think they ice-fish just to get off on the fumes of the gas auger."

But despite the regional differences, Dore believed there was a common thread. To his mind, it's the essential rite of passage for the Canadian male, a shamanistic experience in which initiates strive to achieve an altered state of consciousness by depriving themselves of comfort and ingesting mind-altering substances.

Once they achieve this altered state, they are ready to experience a spiritual catharsis, or at the very least, mild frostbite and a hangover.

"I remember my dad taking me out when I was very young. I was submerged in the company of men, separated by ice and time from all things female. Something was suspended between father and son. At home, I was the son of my father, subject to his domestic rules, his opinions, and lower down on the patriarchal scale. But out on the ice, father and son transcend the hierarchy; I became a younger, less experienced fisherman with an older, more experienced one. And so the conversation would turn on practical matters and telling stories. It was an atmosphere that releases all of us from our usual boring identities."

But even viewed from this angle, ice-fishing is a contradiction. "On the one hand, there's an emphasis on getting back to nature to subject yourself to the power of the great outdoors. On the other hand, you're dressed up in a Ski-Doo suit locked inside your ice shed. The amount of time you actually spend outdoors is minimal, and even then you're so insulated from nature that you can't begin to enjoy it. But in a way, it's the perfect image for Canada. We emphasize our love of nature, when in fact we're an urban country that can't wait to get back to the mall."

By now, we were well north of Montreal proper. We'd already taken one bridge over the arm of the St. Lawrence known as the Rivière des Prairies, a stone's throw from the greatest lake sturgeon spawning grounds in the world, and were approaching the long bridge over Rivière des Mille Îles on the north side of Laval. Coming from the west coast, I'd forgotten how pervasive a presence the St. Lawrence was. No province except Newfoundland is so intimately tied to a body of water. More than 90 percent of Quebeckers live along the banks of the St. Lawrence. Its flow determined the pattern of settlement, the layers of seigneurial land where proximity to the river defined social standing and provided the earliest settlers with communications and transportation links, and an endless supply of fresh water and fish. The river is some 1,840 miles long, third only to the Mackenzie and Yukon rivers in this country, and the largest body of water flowing into the Atlantic. When we reached the other side of the bridge, Lamont turned off onto a side street. As if we'd entered a different country, the urban world melted into the rural. After another twenty minutes along increasingly smaller roads, we crossed a narrow bridge, barely wide enough for Lamont's Deux Chevaux, and abruptly turned off onto a trail in the snow.

"Ah, here we go," he said a moment later, as he stopped the car and shut off the engine.

"Where the hell are we?" Manley asked.

"I have absolutely no idea."

Nearby was a large lake, the size of twenty Olympic stadiums but in much better repair. The lake was dotted with basketball-sized scars in the ice from old fishing holes that had frozen over. One by one, we piled out of the car and unpacked our equipment and provisions. In preparing for this trip, there'd been a bit of a conflict between the two dominant schools of thought. The minimalist school, headed by Manley, suggested that less was more. If we really wanted to enjoy the particular experiences ice-fishing had to offer, her argument went, we should bring only the bare essentials: rods and reels, some tackle, a tarp to cover us and a hand-operated ice auger. The other school of thought, put forth by me and Lamont, was that we should make every effort to be comfortable, and towards that end we'd brought a power auger, a heater and, of course, the makeshift ice shed, which in its glory days had served as a three-seater outhouse on the Dore family farm.

By now a harsh wind was blowing clouds of loose snow across the frozen lake, but the outhouse was surprisingly roomy and comfortable, and as an added bonus, provided us with a wealth of reading material: ancient back issues of French-edition *Chatelaîne* and circa 1960 Sears catalogues. Once inside Ice Station Zebra Mussel, we immediately set to work: Lamont and I diligently endeavoured to uncap our beers without a proper opener, almost ruining the ignition key before realizing they were twist tops, while Lillian Manley operated a small, hand-held cocktail jigger and prepared a kind of high-energy elixir using only rye whiskey and Tang orange-flavour crystals. Once our drinks were in place, Lamont set to the task of cutting a hole in the ice.

"The beauty of ice-fishing is that you don't need a lot of fancy equipment," he shouted over the noise of the gas auger. "The twenty-five-dollar rod and reel from Canadian Tire will work just as well as some of the expensive tilts and traps they're using down in the States. There's no fight in these fish. The oxygen level is so low in the winter that the fish move like zombies; it's sort of like catching corpses. When I ice-fish, I usually have my hook a few centimetres from the bottom, and bounce it on the bottom every now and then. My reasoning is simple: I honestly think that sometimes a fish will strike just because it's bored. There's not a heck of a lot to do down there."

Whitefish and brook trout, perch and walleye—all these are popular among Quebec's ice fishermen. But we'd come for more. We were looking for the giants of central Canada's waters, the big fish of the pike and sturgeon families.

Of all the fish families in the country, none are more cantankerous, ornery or mythical than the pike. They are the bad boys of Canada's lakes and rivers, striking fear in the hearts of children and causing many an angler more than one sleepless night. Of the five species of pike found in Canadian waters, two are the stuff of legend: the northern pike and the monstrous muskellunge. The pike family has an honoured place in fishing lore. These fish are renowned for attaining unbelievable sizes—Pliny reported one weighing more than a thousand pounds, while Konrad von Gesner, a fifteenth-century biologist, told of a nineteen-foot specimen captured and displayed by the monks of Mannheim Cathedral. What's more, the ferocity of the pike is unparalleled in freshwater fish. There's a published report from the 1860s of a fifteen-year-old English boy, identified only as "Longhurst," who was attacked by a giant pike while bathing in a pond; more recently, there's an unsubstantiated report of a man in northern Manitoba whose big toe was "bit clear off" by a northern pike.

Northern pike, or jackfish as they're called in the west, are the smaller of the two. They average eight to ten pounds, although anglers frequently land twenty- and even forty-pounders. They're fierce fighters on the hook—this, along with their long crooked mouth with rows of sharp teeth, has played into the myth of the northern pike as a freshwater barracuda that will as soon attack a fisherman as pass him by. The northern is a long slender fish, with two large fins on the top and bottom of the back of its tail. They are one of the most widespread fish in the world, with a range that extends from northern Europe through to Asia and on to North America. In Canada they can be found almost anywhere there's cool but relatively shallow water, although they seem to favour the waters of Ontario and Quebec. Despite their ferocious image, they are rather sedentary creatures. They like the solitude of the weeds and don't mind waiting for dinner to swim right by. And on the subject of dinner—well, the northern pike just can't seem to get enough, which suits anglers fine. As author and fisherman David Carpenter wrote in *Fishing in the West*, the northern pike is the perfect training fish for the incomplete angler who hasn't "the time or patience to learn the difficult art of trout fishing."

Jackfish are rarely not hungry, and a wiley pike in good waters is about as rare as a talking flounder. Pike eat everything: perch, minnows of all sizes including their own, whitefish, suckers, frogs, snakes, crayfish, leeches, mice, and young waterfowl. In one study of pike, it was found that the weight of their preferred food equalled about 15 percent of their own body weight. That means that huge pike frequently eat fish that weigh 2 to 3 kg or more (about 4 to 8 pounds). Sometimes they rise slowly from their weedy caverns and watch you casting. It makes you wonder . . . just what don't these monsters eat?

Northern pike have been rather mistreated over the years. Because they are both a sport and a commercial fish in most of the country, they have often been overlooked when it came time to draw up the fishing regulations. It's only recently that bag and size limits have been put into effect. It's also got a bad rap as an eating fish, mainly because its scales are covered in a thick mucus, which must be properly removed before you cook the fish. Anglers should also be wary of a tapeworm that often makes its home inside the big pike. If the fish is not properly cooked, the parasite will be happy to relocate inside the gut of a nice fat fisherman.

For those of you who think the northern pike is trouble, watch out for its bigger, meaner cousin, the muskellunge. They're like great big northern pike, although their jaw is straighter and smaller, giving them a kinder, gentler appearance. But don't let their good looks fool you. The muskie—the name comes from an Ojibwa word meaning, what else, "big pike"—is the fiercest fighter in Canada's fresh water, and a perpetual eating machine that will swallow anything that gets in its way, including waterfowl, snakes and small rodents. The average landed muskie weighs about ten pounds, but they can easily reach forty or fifty pounds. A record seventy-pounder was taken out of the St. Lawrence by an angler named Arthur Lawton in 1957, although Scott and Crossman, in *Freshwater Fishes of Canada*, say that muskies have been known to exceed six feet and one hundred pounds. But it's not just the size of the fish that appeals to anglers. The muskie is a difficult quarry that's much less likely to take the hook than its northern cousin. And when it is hooked, it puts on, in Manley's words, "the show of a lifetime." Typically, they strike hard, then take a long, long run. Even when they're hooked and headed to the boat, they don't give up the fight. Veteran anglers shake their heads remembering muskies that escaped the hook seconds before being landed in the boat. The range of the muskellunge is limited to eastern North America, and in Canada it's found mostly in Quebec and Ontario. It's also making inroads in some smaller lakes in Manitoba, although it's not native to the area. Like the northern pike, muskie were once part of the commercial fishery. But since the turn of the century, their popularity as a game fish has prompted various governments to bring in regulations to limit the harvest, leaving the muskie available only to anglers.

The other great monster of Quebec's fresh water is the sturgeon. It's impossible to mistake a sturgeon for any other fish. They have a long sharp body, lacking scales, covered with spiky points and thick, rubbery plates. Their long, pointed nose ends in four barbs surrounding the mouth, which guides them in their search for food. There are five sturgeon species. The shortnose, the baby of the family, rarely exceeds ten pounds and is found only on the Saint John River, in New Brunswick; the rare green sturgeon, found only on Vancouver Island and the Fraser River; the huge white sturgeon of British Columbia; the Atlantic sturgeon, which can be found throughout the St. Lawrence system; and the most common of all, the lake or yellow sturgeon.

Because they live on river and lake bottoms where concentrations of toxins are highest, and due to their slow reproductive cycle—some females do not reach sexual maturity until their twenty-fifth birthday—all sturgeon are at risk, although conservationists are paying special attention to shortnose, green and white sturgeon stocks. The Committee on the Status of Endangered Wildlife in Canada, the agency that monitors the health of fish and other animals in the country, has placed these three sturgeon on their "vulnerable" list.

While all the sturgeon deserve their place in Canadian Fhishstory books, two—the white and lake—stand out. White sturgeon are the largest freshwater fish in Canada, and I do mean large. A record white was caught on the Fraser River near New Westminster in 1897; it weighed 1,387 pounds, dripping wet. There's an unsubstantiated report of an 1,800-pounder taken on the Fraser near Mission a few years earlier. These fish regularly reach twenty feet, but in Canadian waters they run to five or six feet, and have an average weight of a couple hundred pounds. They are unique to the North American side of the Atlantic. Although they are a freshwater fish, preferring murky estuaries, they often move to salt water for a time. White sturgeon are now protected on rivers like the Fraser, although there is a huge underground traffic in them. Poachers can command up to twenty dollars a pound for them on the black market, and face paltry fines if caught, so the illegal catch continues unabated. Like all sturgeon, white are slow to mature. Males do not become sexually active until some time between their eleventh and twenty-second years, while females do not reach maturity until their mid-twenties. Even then, a female will breed only every four years, with the interval expanding up to as much as eleven years as she gets older. It's no wonder, then, that female whites are known to carry up to two hundred pounds of eggs.

Lake sturgeon do not grow to the same bulk as some of their cousins, but they are known to reach fantastic lengths. In 1922, a fisherman hauled a white sturgeon out of Batchewana Bay in Lake Superior that was just short of twelve feet long and weighed in at 310 pounds. Today, the average lake sturgeon runs between three and five feet, and can weigh anywhere from ten to eighty pounds. They're also extremely long-lived. Scientists have identified some specimens they believe to be more than a hundred and fifty years old, although the normal life span is around fifty years for males, eighty for females. They're found throughout Quebec, the Great Lakes and as far west as Alberta. There are rumours that some have even been caught in the Northwest Territories, but scientists have yet to confirm their presence that far north. Today they are a popular sportfish in Quebec, especially within the St. Lawrence watershed. But that wasn't always the case. In the 1800s, fishermen considered the lake sturgeon a waste of precious space, and a threat to equipment. They were routinely killed and dumped back into the water, or kept as pig food or fertilizer—even burned for fuel by steamboats on the Detroit River. Around the turn of the century, people developed a taste for smoked lake sturgeon, and found that their eggs made for an acceptable caviar. Then the kill was really on. In the years 1885 to 1895, fishermen took more than five million pounds of sturgeon from Lake Erie alone, perhaps as much as 90 percent of the available adult stock. Overfishing, pollution and now hydroelectric dams, which cut off the lake sturgeon's traditional migration patterns, led to the decline of this great fish.

Things had not been going well. Lillian Manley and Lamont Dore had argued for one full hour, with barely a break to sip their drinks. The topic was, of course, the whole separation thing. I could have seen it coming. Lamont is an outspoken supporter of the separatist cause, and is usually hauled in by the CBC to provide expert commentary whenever there's another referendum. He believed that the English Canadians, in giving up nationalism in favour of "fast-food global politics," were giving up on the country, and in this sense, separatists were the only true Canadians left. Manley was strictly old-school Britannia, someone who still had a bad taste in her mouth about the loss of the Union Jack. At this troubled stage of her life, she'd been openly flirting with the Reform Party, which Lamont called "a collection of hillbillies, crybabies and fuddy-duddies." Manley disagreed, and not very demurely. Reform was the voice of the people, she said. It was the true champion of the Conservative tradition of Macdonald and Diefenbaker.

"Reformers are conservatives with no sense of nation," Lamont said. "They are Americans in long johns, they are—"

I stopped Lamont short, before he alienated any more readers. He threw up his arms in frustration.

"Once, to be a Canadian meant to build, along with the Québécois, a more ordered and stable society than the Americans. Now that purpose is lost, and the hopes of our two nations have died. We find ourselves," he struggled for the right words, "we find ourselves like fish on the shore of a drying lake. The element necessary to our existence is gone."

Lamont grew silent. Manley by now had completely given up on him and seemed absorbed in her London *Times* crossword puzzle. I didn't know what to say. My political position was clear. I deferred. Perhaps it has something to do with my family history: my mother is French and Irish Catholic; my father, English and

Anglican. I just can't bring myself to take a stand, and in fact, I bend over backwards to make sure I don't step on anyone's toes, culturally speaking. I'm the guy who stewed for twenty minutes over which of the two shirts I had thoughtlessly packed would be less controversial: my Toronto Maple Leafs sweat or my CBC T-shirt. I finally settled on the CBC.

Manley and Dore were not speaking to each other. He was engrossed in his beer, humming "Mon Pays" just loud enough for Manley to hear. She pretended to work on her crossword, although I couldn't help but notice that she never progressed past three words. By now the gas heater was humming along nicely, our lines were set, and all of us had our drinks. I decided to break the ice. I told of the muskie I'd seen as a kid, fishing off my grandfather's boat in Lake Erie; it must have been three and a half feet long, and as it skimmed the surface I could clearly see several fishing hooks embedded in its muzzle. Lamont Dore had a similar story, and remembered being stricken with terror by the sight of the fish, and yanking his line from the water before it could strike. "I was petrified," Dore said. "In that moment, I came to understand the meaning of life, and death."

Lillian Manley, though, saved the best story for last. She was up on Wapawekka Lake, southeast of La Ronge, Saskatchewan, researching a story on a popular fishing resort, the Northern Echo Lodge, when she decided to take off by herself for an afternoon. She'd been fishing in deep water without success, two hours without a single strike, when she decided to move to shallow water close to shore. She settled on a spot and rigged a fly rod for big fish. On her very first cast, a monstrous muskie took the hook. She estimated its size to be anywhere from four and a half to five feet long: "the exact length was impossible to determine because of the angle of refraction off the water." Manley said she played the fish for forty-five minutes and seemed to have won the upper hand. Just as she was bringing it to the boat, she stood up and leaned forward with her net. It was a near fatal mistake. The pike bolted, and Lillian found herself up to her neck in the ice-cold water.

"I decided that the most prudent course of action was to tow the boat to the shore, only some seventy-five or eighty metres away," she said. "I believed that would be safer than trying to re-enter the boat from the water. But I had barely taken a step when I felt something ram into my back. At first, I thought it was my rod, or perhaps just a piece of debris in the water that had been churned up through my activity. But then I was struck again, this time from the side, and with much greater ferocity. I clearly saw my assailant."

As she spoke, Manley unzipped her Ski-Doo suit and began to roll up her shirt sleeve. Her arms were remarkably powerful; years of fishing had left her with thick forearms and biceps that would put a female body-builder to shame. "It was my muskie, still bearing my tackle, seeking its revenge. He took a chunk out of my arm, so great that I still bear the mark of this fish today." Manley held up her arm for us to see. Lamont and I gasped. Just above the elbow was a large cross-shaped scar. "And the strangest part—and you're going to think I'm crazy—but the strangest part is that as the fish swam away, a chunk of my flesh worming its way down his gullet, as he swam away I could have sworn I heard him laugh." Manley paused for a moment, then took a swig of her rye and Tang. "And I can tell you this: a more devilish, insidious laugh I have not heard."

At the exact moment Lillian finished her story, my rod jerked downward and I nearly jumped out of my skin.

"You've got something there," Lamont cried. "Let her run!"

I was beginning to think that "Let her run!" was the only bit of genuine advice fishermen had to offer—like the golfers' all-purpose

"Keep your head down"—but my attention quickly turned to the fish at the end of my rod. My line spun out slowly, as the half-asleep fish tried to wander away from my hook. A moment later, I slowly started to reel in. There was a jerk and the hook set in the fish's jaw; after that, I reeled in steadily, for my quarry had no fight in her. After hauling the fish for two or three minutes, a small pike's head emerged from the frigid water. It was already unconscious, having exhausted itself with its meagre fight. I had finally caught a fish.

Lamont hauled it up onto the ice and it lay there for a moment. I half expected it to jump up, leap into the water and swim for safety, keeping my perfect record intact. But it did not move. Lamont gave it a crack on the head with the preacher just to make sure it was dead. It wasn't a huge fish. Fifteen inches long and, by Manley's estimation, two pounds. And while the rest of the crew were toasting my success and slapping me on the back, I must admit to a certain remorse. I had waited all these years to catch a fish, but the experience itself turned out to be a letdown. Besides, what had this poor fish ever done to me? What right did I have to take its life? I put on a game face, and tried to keep these thoughts to myself, but Lamont, who's always been a sensitive type, knew something was up. He put his arm around my shoulder, in a consoling kind of way. "Murderer," he whispered. I excused myself. I needed a few moments to clear my head, and get used to my new life as a successful fisherman.

Another Gratuitous Catch Scene

Nothing could have prepared me for what I encountered when I returned to the rotting outhouse that served as our shelter from the elements. Manley and Dore were naked, except for their Ski-Doo boots, sprawled on the makeshift bench, locked in a frenzied, animal embrace.

Dore was murmuring something in French, which, thankfully, I didn't understand; Lillian Manley tittered like a schoolgirl, then dug her nails into Dore's flabby back.

"Ah . . . excuse me," I mumbled, and turned to go.

"Chris! Wait!" Dore called. "We've got some wonderful news." He beamed at Manley. "Honey, you tell him."

Manley fluttered her eyes and tilted her head. "We're moving to Florida. We're going to open a fish farm. We're getting married!"

"And, mon ami, *we owe it all to you."*

Chapter 9

Sorry, Charlie

An old docker with gutted cheeks,
time arrested in the used-up-knuckled hands
crossed on his lap, sits
in a spell of the glinting water.

He dreams of times in the cider sunlight
when masts stood up like stubble;
but now a gull cries, lights,
flounces its wings ornately, folds them,
and the waves slop among the weed-grown piles.

"Charlottetown Harbour," by Milton Acorn

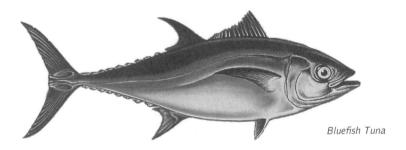

Bluefish Tuna

*Not catching tuna in Wedgeport, Nova Scotia,
former Tuna Capital of the World*

I f you drive three and a half hours south from Halifax along the eastern shore, just shy of Yarmouth, you'll come to a little finger of Nova Scotia sticking out into the no-man's waters between the Atlantic Ocean and the Bay of Fundy. Take a left and drive to the very end, and there you'll find the community of Wedgeport. You'll know you're there when you pass the Knights of Columbus building and A.L. LeBlanc's gas station. It's Acadian country down here, everybody speaks French, and English too, and every second person you meet is named LeBlanc. In the heart of this 230-year-old village of quaint, clapboard houses and modest shops is the brand spanking new, seven-thousand-square-foot million-dollar-plus Wedgeport Tuna Fishing Museum and Interpretive Centre. It's a fascinating memorial to the days when this village was one of the most famous sporting spots in Canada. Before most people outside of the country had heard of the Stanley Cup, they knew about Wedgeport's International Tuna Competition, the premier sporting event of its day.

A late spring rain had just started to fall as I pulled into the museum parking lot. A couple of middle-aged women in Lycra pants power-walked past me and cut across the lawn of the Wedgeport Retired Fishermen's Association right next door. Standing by the door was Rosalee Hattie, my volunteer tour guide for the morning. Rosalee had lived in Wedgeport all her life, and remembered the heyday of the Tuna Cup from when she was a little girl.

"It was always in September, after school had started," she told me as she unlocked the door to the museum. "Every afternoon after the bell, all us girls would run home and change into our pants and come down to the wharf. It was so strange to be one day in this little Acadian town in the middle of nowhere, and the next day to be in the centre of the universe. You have to remember, in those days the Tuna Cup was as popular as the World Series."

The whole idea of Wedgeport fascinated me. First, I'd never heard of it, and I'm always happy to find a part of Canada's popular history that's slipped from the national consciousness. Second, I'm enthralled with any aspect of Maritime identity. My wife's mother's family comes from Cape Breton Island, so we get to spend a lot of time on the east coast. And coming from British Columbia, where the closest we get to genuine culture is our morning bowl of yogurt, I like the Gaelic sensibility that runs through the province.

Rosalee Hattie comes from true blue—or should I say, bluefin? —Wedgeport stock. Her great-uncle Évée LeBlanc was one of the most prominent tuna captains—in fact, the very first. Her grandparents had run an inn called the Fishermen's Rest, a popular hangout for tuna tourists. Her mother had worked at the inn, and after she got married, she started taking tourists into her own home. So Rosalee grew up surrounded by the world of big-game fishing. Because of her background, she got involved with the Wedgeport museum society back in 1991, and set about preserving the village's glory days, which started quite by accident in 1936 and ended with a thud twenty-two years later.

Today, seventeen hundred people live in Wedgeport, and lobster fishing is the main industry. Things weren't much different sixty years ago, when an American millionaire sportsman named Michael Lerner rolled into town with his wife, Helen. They were en route from a swordfishing jaunt in Cape Breton to the Boston-bound steamship out of Yarmouth when they pulled into Wedgeport to gas up. Back then, there were about a thousand people living in the area, and the fishery was for herring and lobster. In the summer, the men would go out and harpoon tuna. The big fish were one big pain in the ass. It took hours to land one, and brought in only three cents a pound at the cannery. The fishermen hated them. They scared off the herring and wrecked the fine mesh nets. Lerner heard a couple of old-timers complaining about those damned tuna and he was immediately intrigued. The next day he hired local boat-builder John LeBlanc to make a swivel chair, a must for the serious big-game fisherman, and hired Évée LeBlanc's lobster boat for the day. "None of the fishermen would believe that anyone would actually pay them to go fishing for tuna with a rod and reel," Rosalee said. "It was unheard of."

But Lerner wasn't quite as crazy as the locals thought. In fact, there was already an established sportfishery for tuna in Liverpool, halfway along the road to Halifax. That all started back in 1871 when a bored teacher named Thomas Patillo decided to have a little fun. He got himself two hundred feet of handline and wound it around a reel. Then he bent a large pin into the shape of a hook. Thus equipped, he pushed in his dory in search of what the locals called "horse mackerel" or "albacore." Within the hour, Patillo hooked into a giant tuna, and the teacher set off on the ride of his life. Remember, he was trying to haul the fish in by hand, without a rod or proper reel. He might have finished out his days being hauled around Liverpool Bay by that giant tuna if he wasn't accidentally pulled through a cluster of herring boats. Needless to say, the fishermen were none too happy having this landlubber disrupt their work. One of them cut Patillo's line, and the disappointed teacher rowed to shore, to a chorus of curses. All was not lost, though. A little while later, Patillo refined his technique and landed himself a six-hundred-pound bluefin. The Maritimes had found a new recreational pastime.

But no one had ever tried such nonsense in Wedgeport, and so there were quite a few doubters in the crowd on the dock the morning Évée LeBlanc took Lerner and his wife out. The captain had seen tuna jump near Soldiers Rip, a mile-long tide stream ten miles outside of Wedgeport, and pointed his boat in that direction. When they reached the rip, Lerner got into a dory tied to the stern of the lobster boat and set his tackle. Not long afterward, he got a strike and LeBlanc, as ordered, cut the dory loose. "They just cut the rope and let the tuna drag the dory until the tuna got tired out. Can you imagine how dangerous that must have been?"

That afternoon, Lerner caught two tuna on rod and reel, much to the amazement of the locals, who carefully inspected the fish on the dock, looking for harpoon holes. The locals were even more amazed when they saw Évée LeBlanc's prize: twenty-five bucks for the boat rental, plus a ten-dollar tip, and the fish thrown into the bargain.

The following Sunday Lerner was joined by another angler, the perfectly named S. Kip Farrington, Jr. I can see him in my mind, in his pith helmet and safari suit, chatting up the local Acadians with his Ivy League–accented Parisienne French. Kip was a well-known sportsman and author. The appearance of the Americans caused quite a stir in town. Within a few minutes of hitting the water, Lerner landed a 275-pound tuna, and followed that up almost immediately with a 390-pounder. Kip followed suit with a baby of 165 pounds, and even Mrs. Farrington got into the act and will live forever in the history books as the first woman to catch a tuna at Wedgeport. Farrington and Lerner quickly realized they'd stumbled upon one of the greatest gamefishing sites in the world. They'd already been thinking of hosting a great game fish tournament, and, thanks to their accidental discovery of Wedgeport, they'd found the perfect spot.

The locals had thought Michael Lerner quite batty when he told them that people the world over would soon be streaming into Wedgeport, to fish the amazing Soldiers Rip. But come they did, and brought with them pockets full of money. A guide could earn a dollar a day, plus tips—good money in those days, and by the 1950s captains were pulling forty dollars a day for boat rentals, if there was a toilet on board, and even more if tackle was included. The annoying tuna were now at the heart of a sportfishing industry that brought $200,000 a year into Wedgeport.

The focus of the summer's festivities was the International Tuna Cup Match, which brought anglers from around the world to Wedgeport's docks. The first Tuna Cup was held in 1937. Kip captained the American team, while the British squad was made up of four wealthy Nova Scotians. The final score saw the tough British side outscore the tenacious Yanks four fish to one in the midst of near-hurricane conditions. The rules were fairly straightforward. Teams were limited to three men, and fishermen had to land their fish in their own boat. They were limited to number 39 thread line of any length they chose, and were free to use any style rod. They also allowed fifteen-foot leaders, and many anglers opted for good old piano wire. Teams got one point per pound of tuna, with daily bonus points for the biggest fish and highest total catch. The following year, Cuba was added to the list of competitors, and the Americans won an impressive victory with their eighteen catches.

By 1953, the Tuna Cup was a truly international event, with wealthy playboys from eight countries as far away as Brazil, Sweden and France joining the fray. The province took control of the tournament and provided room and board and boats for competitors, because of the international publicity it generated. Bolstered by Lerner and Farrington's social connections, the Tuna Match quickly became world-renowned; celebrities like President Roosevelt, writer Zane Grey and boxer Gene Tunney fished there; Ernest Hemingway himself was on the Honorary Board of Governors. For two weeks every September, the tiny village of Wedgeport was magically transformed into the most cosmopolitan city on earth. Each year, the tuna dock was, as David MacDonald wrote in the September 17, 1955, edition of *Maclean's*, "aflutter with bunting and the babble of French, Spanish and English, a kilted piper waits to skirl boats in from the sea and red-coated Mounties hold back gay holiday crowds. It is a time of parties, when Acadian fishermen sip Martinis with Brazilian coffee kings, when a Cuban tries to teach Mme. Israel Pothier to samba and when Father Adolph LeBlanc is happy, but not surprised, to find a fifty-dollar bill in St. Michael's poor box."

Sportsmanship of the kind never found today was the rule at the Tuna Cup tournaments. MacDonald reports that violations of the unwritten code were almost never heard of. Once, an uncouth American cut a Cuban angler's line when it came too near his boat—but the Cuban did not raise the red protest flag. Afterwards, when his teammates learned what he'd done, the American was cut loose from the team and never invited back. The only reported incidence of the red flag being raised was back in the early 1950s. It was raised by a man named Louis Mowbray of the British Empire team. "I want to complain about these Nova Scotians," he yelled to the tournament officials as they hove into hearing range.

The officials were nervous; they didn't want a whiff of scandal to sully the competition. "Which Nova Scotians?" the judge asked.

"The tuna," replied Mowbray. "They won't take my hook."

In Wedgeport, Nova Scotia's tourism department had found the perfect product. A quaint fishing community, blessed with an unbelievably abundant natural resource, was visited each year by the world's richest and most celebrated outdoorsmen, who cherished, above all else, the ancient rituals and codes of good sportsmanship. Everything came to a head in 1949. That year, angling teams from Britain, the United States, Brazil, Argentina and

Cuba caught a record seventy-two tuna, with a combined weight of 27,161 pounds. It was the end of a dream season that saw 1,760 bluefin landed. Things were only getting better, and as the world wondered if there was any limit to Wedgeport's bounty, some of the more cynical locals wondered when would it all come crashing down.

Lillian Manley has a different take. She calls tuna fishing—all big-game fishing—the "highest form of the lowest order of angling." The whole point, as she explained it, was to hook on to one of these monsters with the most heavy-duty equipment possible, then have the fish haul you and your boatload of friends around for four or five hours, until it was too tired to blink. "Where's the sport in that?" Manley complained. "Why don't you just shoot the thing, and put it out of its misery quickly?"

If you drive an hour south from Halifax, in a region the tourist brochures call the Light House Route, you'll come to an area of green rolling hills and farmland. In the heart of this region sits the town of Lunenburg, noted for its striking, turn-of-the-century architecture, and long history as a commercial fishing centre. According to B.A. Balcom's *History of the Lunenburg Fishing Industry*, published by the local marine museum in 1977, the town was founded in the 1750s, when Britain, looking for a way to counter French settlement in the region, brought over groups of German-speaking Protestants from southwestern Germany, the Montbéliard district of France, and Switzerland and Holland. The Brits selected a place fifty miles south of Halifax that the French called

Mirligeuche. It had a good, deepwater harbour, and some of the best farmland on the eastern shore. It was also protected to the north by a long peninsula, which made the settlement easy to defend against French raids. Because of the fertile soil, the Lunenburg settlers first turned to agriculture as a basis of their economy. They also developed forestry, providing Halifax with firewood and timber for boat-building.

By the 1790s, the Lunenburg settlers had a thriving economy, and some wanted to branch out into other industries. The fishery was a natural, and a group of the town's successful entrepreneurs decided to try fishing as a way to expand their financial empires. There were some limitations, though. The Lunenburg schooners had to travel great distances to the best cod waters, and that limited them to brief jaunts in April, May and October. It was an expensive proposition, and while a good trip meant a schooner would come back with its hold stuffed full of cod, a bad trip was a financial shipwreck for the owners. By 1829, Lunenburg had quite a substantial fishing fleet, numbering thirty-two vessels, not including dories.

Part of the growth was due to subsidies from the Nova Scotia government in what amounted to the first make-work project on the continent. In order to capture a suitable share of the European and South American salt fish trade, Halifax offered a bounty to encourage larger vessels to go after the big cod runs off Labrador and Newfoundland. Big boats meant more work for Nova Scotians. A typical trip for the Lunenburg fleet went something like this. Come June, they'd set out for the coast of Labrador. Once they'd established their base, they'd fish for capelin, that member of the smelt family that served as bait fish for the cod industry. Once they had enough bait, the ships would anchor in a safe harbour, store their sails and rigging, and get ready to do some serious fishing. The work itself was done from dories manned by three or four men with handlines. Meanwhile, there'd be a couple of crews of men working on board to process the cod, gutting them and cutting off their heads, tails and fins before packing them in barrels full of salt. When the ship had enough cod, the fish would be taken to shore to dry in the sun. For the fishermen and crew, it was a miserable job. In his wonderful book *Images of Lunenburg County*, historian and photographer Peter Barss interviewed many of the old-timers who'd been to the Labrador banks between the wars, and had experienced a way of life that had changed little in one hundred years. One unidentified fisherman remembered those days with little fondness.

> Dory fishing was disgustin'—a disgustin' job. A fearful disgustin' job. To go down there in that hold with the frost hanging down—icicles hangin' down o'erhead from the deck planks. Go down there to bait up five tubs of gear to a dory. And you stayed down there till you had it baited up—till the cook blowed the whistle for breakfast about half past two or three o'clock in the mornin'. . . . You'd be sittin' down in the fo'c's'cle—when the wind was blowin' a good breeze—an' maybe you couldn't get right off—waitin' with your gear all baited up, not daylight yet, dark and waitin'. Laying round wet and in your oil clothes on. And waitin' for a feller to come along and sing out, "Get up your tubs, boys!" Couldn't take your oil clothes off on account of there might be a set in the next minute—the next minutes, the next half hour—waitin' for that . . .
>
> Then when the call did come, you'd hoist the dories out an' hang 'em out o'er the side. An' if you was on the wind'ard side—more than once I shut my eyes. The fellers on the deck would let the dory fly. If the vessel made a roll to the leeward you was up about twenty feet. An' if you fetched up against

the vessel—if your tongue was between your teeth, you'd bite your tongue off. . . . Then you had a course to row. If the wind was blowin' west, you'd set out an' go maybe sou'east. That's right off the wind. In the dark! Well, you'd make your run down an' if you find the buoy, fine. But, if you didn't find your buoy, you'd go back to the vessel an' go again. An' sometimes if it was fog t'ick or blowin', you'd make maybe two, three trips before you'd find your trawl buoy; a mile down and a mile back. Four hauls a day wit' several miles o' gear ahead o' you. Sometimes it wasn't so good. An' after you made your last haul of the day an' all them fish was forked up on the deck, why then you'd go to work an' help the dress gang get the fish split an' salted down. An' if you was getting any amount o' fish, why you had some pile of work ahead o' you.

Lunenburg peaked fast. Its Golden Age was in the early 1830s, but overly eager entrepreneurs expanded too quickly. In 1835, the local insurance collective failed, and the fishery took a hit. As a reaction, fishermen started to diversify their catch, looking less to cod and more to fish like herring and mackerel. But these changes were not without problems, and the New-foundland fishermen in particular were not happy with these Lunenburg upstarts moving in on their traditional fish stocks. One incident in the fall of 1886 brought everything to a head. Two Lunenburg boats, the *Willet* and the *Water Lily*, were seine fishing for herring off Labrador when a mob of four hundred angry Newfies attacked. They wrecked the seine nets and set on the Lunenburg crew, who were lucky to escape with their lives. The attack prompted Halifax to ask London for help. The Brits promptly sent a warship out to protect the Nova Scotian crews; it arrived two weeks late in a port two hundred miles south of the herring fishing grounds.

In the 1870s the Maritime fishery began to unravel, although Lunenburg, because of its diverse economy and unique cultural history, was better insulated than most communities. The beginning of the end was the introduction of the powerful trawl schooners. Previously, fishermen would bait a line the night before, then during the day, haul it into a dory several times to re-bait and re-set it. But a Lunenburg captain named Ben Anderson came up with an improved method: he called it "underrunning," and it was a system that allowed fishermen to progress back and forth through a line, removing fish and re-baiting as they went along. These long haul lines carried hundreds of hooks, and required more bait not just to set the lines, but to replace the last bait. And while handlines tended to attract larger fish, these trawl lines caught everything in their path. The results were fewer capelin, so less food for the cod, and the loss of younger fish, who hadn't yet spawned.

The decline continued into the new century with the advent of the gas engine and the otter trawlers, powerful ships with ravenous nets. On top of everything else, the industry itself had become more efficient and mobile, and countries that had to rely on the fishermen of Newfoundland and Nova Scotia could go out and catch their own fish. Great Britain and Norway offered subsidies to help build up their fish fleets and specifically targeted Nova Scotian markets in Central and South America; Norway, for example, flat out paid Cuba $600,000 to buy its fish.

The Depression only fuelled the growing fish crisis, especially in Newfoundland where the outport mentality resisted all efforts to modernize and diversify the fishery. By 1939, virtually all of Canada's Atlantic groundfish were caught out of four Nova Scotian ports: Halifax, Lunenburg, North Sydney and Lockeport. Finally, our old friend refrigeration bared its icy claws; while a boon to fresh fish lovers the world over, the rise of refrigeration marked the death of the salt fish trade. Nova Scotia was quicker than most to pick up on this new processing phenomenon, but it was still a time of great turmoil in the fishing industry.

I find it interesting that as the fishery faded things like the Wedgeport Tuna Tournament and the Dennis Cup, the international race in which Lunenburg's *Bluenose I* earned her reputation as the fastest schooner on the water, captured the public's imagination. Maybe it was just a case of how history repeats itself first as tragedy, then as comedy—or, more recently, as the CBC movie of the week. Or maybe it was just part of an unspoken understanding we had reached with the fish, one last celebration of them and the lifestyle they supported before they disappeared completely. At the turn of the century, there were 150 fish boats operating out of Lunenburg, and the town's shipbuilders were working around the clock to maintain the largest fishing fleet of any Canadian port; ten years later, the Lunenburg fleet was down to a hundred ships. By the end of the First World War there were only a handful left, and most of those made more money running rum than chasing fish. And what's left? Today, Lunenburg is a United Nations World Heritage Site, its old docks and fish sheds restored and protected as a monument to the way things were. History. Tragedy. Tourism.

The International Tuna Cup put Wedgeport and Nova Scotia on the world's tourist maps, and the provincial government was quick to take full advantage of the publicity. During the forties and fifties, the Nova Scotia tourism department spent more on promoting Wedgeport than they spent on any other single attraction or event. It's hard to overstate the importance that tourism during this time had in shaping our modern idea of the "traditional" Nova

Scotian, and the Maritime way of life. It's around this time that Nova Scotia began to deliberately cultivate an image of being North America's rustic, rather Scottish Shangri-La, full of simple fisherfolk and their dories and oilskins. Undaunted by simple facts like the predominance of people from British and Yankee heritage in the province, and the historical supremacy of industry over fisheries—even as far back as the 1880s, fishermen made up less than 10 percent of Nova Scotia's workforce—the provincial government trawled on, selling Nova Scotia's invented innocence to middle-class Americans and Europeans ever jaded by world wars, the Depression and the ceaseless march of progress.

Wedgeport's days in the sun ended as suddenly as they started. In 1958, only one bluefin was caught in the whole season, and the Tuna Cup organizers, good sports that they were, decided to put the match on hold. The following year, the tuna turned up off Cape St. Mary, just around the corner from Wedgeport at the mouth of the Bay of Fundy. For some reason they had changed their migratory patterns, normal practice for tuna, which follow the warmest currents to the best food supplies. The tuna captains shifted their operations southwest, and the match was on again. But the contest was losing its magic. By the late sixties, tuna catches off southwestern Nova Scotia had dwindled: three in 1966; two in 1967; none in 1969. The fish had moved again, to the waters off Prince Edward Island. But in 1965, the big fish returned without warning, and the International Tuna Cup Match continued for another ten years until the tuna run dried up for good. There were half-hearted attempts to get an all-Canadian tournament up and running—it was sponsored first by Benson & Hedges 100s, and then by, who else, Labatt. But it never caught on like the big fish tournaments in the good old days.

The bluefin tuna is the largest member of the mackerel family and, after the Pacific black marlin, the second largest game fish in the world. Bluefin grow as much as fourteen feet long and reach a weight of one ton. The largest ever caught at Wedgeport weighed in at a svelte 1,148 pounds, and was taken on harpoon; no Nova Scotia angler ever broke the 1,000-pound barrier, but a retired army officer from Montreal named Duncan Hodgson came very close. In September of 1950, he caught a 977-pounder off St. Ann Bay, Nova Scotia. Harvey Teller, a San Francisco businessman, holds the record for the biggest bluefin caught by rod and reel at Wedgeport. In 1951, he landed a 932-pounder.

Bluefin are only one of five tuna species found in the Maritime waters; the others are yellowfin, bigeye, blackfin and albacore, the name still used by some old-timers when referring to bluefin. The adult bluefin fits the image of the classic tuna; its streamlined body, distinguished by ridges along the back of its tail, and a huge caudal fin helps power the fish to speeds in excess of fifty miles an hour. The Wedgeport tuna originated from an area known as the Great Bahama Bank, fifty miles east of Miami in the Caribbean Sea. It takes them three weeks to move northward, past the New England states, up to Nova Scotia. In these cooler waters, their thoughts move from migration to feeding, and the hunger is on. They feast on mackerel, squid, herring—virtually any small fish they can sink their teeth into.

I wasn't surprised when Rosalee said none of the fishermen she knew ever followed the tourists in their gentlemanly pursuit of the big tuna; for the men of Wedgeport in particular, it must have seemed like the ultimate busman's holiday. But then, Maritimers in general have had an ambivalent relationship with sportfishing. Today less than 8 percent of Nova Scotians are anglers, which puts the people of this province at the bottom of the list in terms of participation in this sport. What's interesting is that, as the province becomes more urbanized and further removed from its fishing heritage, the proportion of anglers has not increased. Much of the reason for this is the lack of a dominant sportfish to capture the public's imagination. Since the tuna ran out, no single fish has swum to the forefront. There are some salmon, but their numbers are limited, their stocks protected, and they're really more a feature of New Brunswick culture. There are some trout, perch and bass in Nova Scotia's freshwater lakes and streams, and some people do angle for groundfish like cod and pollock—but that's the last resort for only the most obsessive fisherman. These days, the brightest light in the darkness of Nova Scotia's sport-fishery is none other than the shark. Specifically, anglers are hunting blue shark, and to a much lesser extent, porbeagle and mako sharks. There are a handful of charter companies who cater to those anglers interested in something a little different, and willing to part with eight hundred bucks. Peter Murphy runs Halifax Harbour Charters, out of Murphy's On the Water Restaurant on the public wharfs. He says that although there's been an increase in the shark fishery over the last couple of years, it's actually been around for some time.

"It's a growing industry, not only from a sportfishing point of view, but from a commercial one as well," Murphy told me as we sat in his family's restaurant. "There's a lot of interest in sharks as other species start to dwindle. And one of the biggest delicacies for the Japanese market is shark fin soup. As a matter of fact, there are a few sharking operations that run out of here. All they used to do was go out, catch the fish, cut the fin off and throw the shark back. A lot of local people don't even realize the abundance of sharks in our waters, especially in the summertime when the waters warm up. You can catch them right in Halifax Harbour. Even great whites are not unheard of down in the southern part of the province."

Despite the growing popularity, Murphy thinks the shark fishery has already peaked. The problem is that there just aren't that many anglers or big-game fishermen who make their way to Halifax. And for the locals, it's more a novelty than anything else.

"It's pretty expensive when you compare it to other similar recreational activities. In fact, what we charge is on par with what the Americans are asking for shark fishing down south. I think the growth is as much due to the desperation of some of the guys running charters as it is anything else. Shark fishing, and the whole charter boat industry in general, has grown over the last few years because of the downturn in the fishing industry; a lot of guys are just trying to supplement their income. But it's tough going. It's not like on the west coast, where fishing guides and whale watching tours can run year round. We have such a short season that it takes a long time just to earn back your initial investment on the boat and equipment."

Like Nova Scotia, Prince Edward Island has never had the strongest recreational fishery. However, on a per capita basis, sportfishing is more popular on the Island than in many other areas of the Maritimes, and it's no wonder. There's a fine selection of freshwater and saltwater fish, from the native brook trout to rainbow trout, which were introduced to the Island in 1925, and even a few Atlantic salmon. Mackerel are a favourite catch on the ocean, and there's even a popular winter ice-fishery for smelt. In the late 1960s, anglers started turning up on Prince Edward Island looking for tuna. The biggest one landed was an 855-pounder in 1967; nine years later, big-game fishermen hauled 680 bluefin out of Prince Edward Island waters. While the fishery enjoyed a brief heyday as bluefin central, the tuna quickly declined.

What distinguishes Prince Edward Island's fishery from any other in the country, though, is the balance that's been struck between recreational and commercial fisheries. With the kind of comradeship not seen outside a few lakes in northern Saskatch-ewan, the fishermen of Prince Edward Island share their resources with little argument. It helps that the main commercial fishery is built around the lobster, a shellfish that is illegal—and flat-out dangerous—for sport fishermen to catch. Still, the anglers stay out of the lobstermen's way from early June to the end of November, when the lobstermen clear out and let the anglers have their turn.

Of all the Maritime provinces, New Brunswick has the strongest sportfishing tradition. Maybe it's because New Brunswick decided to diversify early in its history and quickly found that things like forestry and agriculture provided a much more stable economic base than fishing. While there are valuable fisheries like scallops along the Georges Bank and the Bay of Fundy purse seine fishery, New Brunswick has traditionally had the lowest proportion of its labour force involved in fisheries; even as far back as the 1880s, fishermen accounted for less than 2 per-cent of all workers. Today, they account for 1 percent of the total. The latest figures from the Department of Fisheries and Oceans show that there are just under 8,700 licensed fishermen in New Brunswick. That compares to 15,500 in Nova Scotia and some 20,100 on The Rock. Even tiny Prince Edward Island, with a pop-ulation nine times smaller than that of New Brunswick, has 5,000 fishermen. Because they don't *have* to fish, people in New Brunswick are more apt to fish for fun. In fact, nearly 10 percent of New Brunswick's 930,000 residents take part in the sport every year. By far the most popular fish among these anglers is the Atlantic salmon. These fish are a breed apart from their Pacific cousins. First, they come in only one flavour. And the size and weight range is limited. Most adults weigh in the vicinity of three to twenty pounds, although sixty-pounders are not uncommon. In appearance, they're probably closer to the chinook than anything else, although Atlantics have a longer snout, and their bottom jaw curls up in a sharp hook. The biggest difference is that the Pacific salmon spawn once and die, whereas the Atlantic salmon often survive the rigours of the spawn.

There are two main stock groups of Atlantic salmon: those that originate in North America and those from Europe. Of the North American fish, the vast majority come from rivers and streams along Canada's east coast. Philip Lee, in *Home Pool: The Fight to Save the Atlantic Salmon,* calls the Miramichi River in New Brunswick the single most important Atlantic salmon base in the world, outproducing all of Iceland's celebrated salmon streams combined.

The Atlantic salmon has always been popular among commercial fishermen and anglers. But in the 1950s scientists discovered that the vast stocks of the North American salmon fed off the west coast of Greenland. At first, only local fishermen were interested, but over the next decade the fishery grew as ships from Canada, Britain, Spain and Russia joined in the hunt. The world should have known better. If nothing else, the Atlantic salmon had already proved itself to be unusually sensitive to overfishing and habitat destruction. In Europe, pollution and hydroelectric dams had wiped out vast salmon reserves on major rivers like the Thames and Rhine in a matter of a few decades, while the North American stocks fared no better in high-use areas like the Great Lakes. By the 1970s, Atlantic salmon were disappearing, and many conservationists were alarmed that these fish would soon become extinct. The commercial salmon fishery on the east coast was devastated, particularly on the Miramichi watershed. In 1967, fishermen pulled 1.4 million pounds of salmon out of New Brunswick's waters; the next year, they took half that amount, and by 1971 the catch was down to less than 270,000 pounds. The Canadian government cut back the number of commercial salmon licences, and soon followed with a scheme to buy back as many licences as possible. About a third of the fishermen took the bait, and they were the lucky ones; in 1972, the DFO closed the Atlantic salmon fishery. When the fishery reopened in 1982, there were 225 fishermen left in New Brunswick, and half of those were on the Miramichi. It seemed the government had been overly optimistic about the health of the stocks, as fishermen found the salmon too scarce and landed less than half of the fifty-thousand-pound quota. In 1985, Ottawa shut the commercial salmon fishery in the Maritimes, although Labrador's fishermen carry on, and as recently as 1995, were catching some fifty-five tons of wild salmon a year.

In the face of the widespread commercial exploitation, the recreational salmon fishery on the east coast persevered. The 1971 changes to the commercial fishery were echoed in changes to the sportfishery. Anglers, who'd enjoyed relative freedom up until then, now faced a two-fish-a-day limit and were restricted to a much smaller fishing area. Then in 1983 the government changed the fishery to catch-and-release only. That set off a mini revolt led by New Brunswick's most serious anglers. They were up in arms because they were paying the price for what they saw as a problem created and perpetuated by the commercial fishing interests, who, unlike anglers, had no real ownership over the resource. You see, alone among the provinces, New Brunswick awarded people ownership over rivers and their contents. In other words, if you owned property bordering on a stream or creek, you were responsible for the upkeep of that portion of the stream, and in turn had exclusive rights to catch any fish that swam through your portion. As well as these entrenched property rights, the provincial government also leases fishing rights on public land, and the bidding on some of the better fishing holes can reach millions of dollars.

This system is a throwback to life in the Old World, where the concept of private ownership over rivers is still widely accepted.

When the settlers first came to New Brunswick, particularly to those areas too wild to readily support any kind of agriculture, the Crown granted them fishing rights to ensure a steady source of food. Today, almost half of New Brunswick's river shores are privately owned, and almost 10 percent of the remaining frontage is leased. While this curious system seems rather undemocratic to the typical Canadian, it has its advantages. Above all, owners and lease holders have a legal responsibility to keep their river in good repair and do what they can to replenish fish stocks. They also have the right to sue anyone who damages their portion of river, a right that even allows them to take industrial polluters to court—a course governments in this country have been reluctant to follow.

The Tuna Cup matches officially ended in 1975, although they've been revived of late in Canso, Nova Scotia, home to the annual Stan Rogers Music Festival. Canso, on the northeastern shore, is the last place in the province with any tuna fishery to speak of, and while the stocks are very low and access is severely restricted—anglers must be accompanied by a licensed commercial fisherman—the payoff can be high. According to Rosalee Hattie, the bluefin were now a delicacy in Japan, and a fisherman could get as much as twenty-four dollars a pound for a whole tuna.

"After the tuna ran out here, some of the folks tried fishing out at Newfoundland," Rosalee remarked to me as my morning at Wedgeport's Sport Tuna Museum was coming to a close. "One fellow told me that when they landed the tuna on the wharf there, women would come up with knives and forks and cut big chunks out of them for dinner. The only time we'd seen chunks out of tuna here is when the sharks had been at them."

I thanked Rosalee for her help and walked out to my rented car. The sun had decided to put in an appearance, and down at the end of the wharf I could see a group of tourists by the small ship that would take them out on a nature tour of the nearby islands, culminating in a lobster and clam bake on St. Martin Island. Suddenly, I had a great idea for my book. I'd tell the story of how I talked a lobster captain into taking me out to Soldiers Rip, how we chummed the water with herring, and then, after strapping myself to the captain's chair, I threw my line into the water. Minutes later, my story would go, the water would be boiling with tuna, and it wasn't long before I got my first strike.

I was surprised how gently the tuna took the bait. He seemed almost to suck it in, taste it delicately, swirling it around in his mouth to capture its vintage and the colour of its palate. The next instant, he took my line with the force of a thundercloud, bursting forth in a run that tore off two hundred yards of line in a matter of seconds. . . .

But no. I decided there'd be no tall fish tales from Wedgeport. I was almost at the end of my Royal Fishin' Commission. It had been a long, hard run, and I was almost out of gas. I missed my family terribly, as the homing instinct settled in. Nope. No more tall tales. Just Newfoundland. Then home. A seagull landed on the hood of my car, a broken lobster claw in his mouth. I watched as he picked away at the slivers of meat some hungry tourist had overlooked, I watched in silence and waited, waited in silence for the next chapter to begin.

Chapter 10

The Chapter That Got Away

I's the b'y that builds the boat,
And I's the b'y that sails her!
I's the b'y that catches the fish
And takes 'em home to Liza . . .
  "I's the B'y," Newfoundland's unofficial national anthem

Capelin

Just about done, in Petty Harbour, Newfoundland

I t looks just like a picture from a postcard: a clutch of wood, clinging to the rock face that surrounds a small bay. In fact, it is a picture postcard of sorts. Petty Harbour, a historic fishing village nine miles south of St. John's, is one of the most photographed spots in Newfoundland, if not the country. It's not the greatest place for a harbour; submerged rocks pose a threat to anyone unfamiliar with the water, while the flow in the bay can cause some heavy swells. But it's been used by Europeans for five hundred years now. Basque fishermen undoubtedly set down at Petty Harbour decades before John Cabot reached the New World, and during the 1600s it was a favourite hangout for privateers—licensed pirates, similar to today's cable companies—who'd sit in wait for ships heading to St. John's. Despite the plans of the Bristol merchants, who didn't want to risk their monopoly by allowing anyone to live on Newfoundland, settlers moved into Petty Harbour, and by the 1670s, the village included five homesteads. And in the decades to come, Petty Harbour grew to an important fishing community, although less an outport than a satellite of St. John's.

I'd come to Petty Harbour to get away from the tourists. I wanted to be by myself, to look at the ocean and consider the fish for one last time. It was to be the very last stop on my Royal Fishin' Commission, on a trip that had taken me from the birthplace of sportfishing in Canada, to this village, not far from the spot where fishing, and the country itself, began. Why Petty Harbour? I'd run into a fellow in town who was knowledgeable in the ways of Newfoundland's fish and fishermen. His name, I kid you not, was Cabot Martin. He was a lawyer and author, and I'd actually picked up his book *No Fish and Our Lives*—about the failure of the cod fisheries—at H.P. Tergesen & Sons' general store in Gimli.

He's the one who suggested I go to Petty Harbour. "It's the picture postcard image of Newfoundland," he said. "It's the place
where all the tourists go."

But there were no tourists today. They were all in Bonavista,
snapping pictures of the *Matthew*, or visiting the Ryan Premises
National Historic Site, a restored nineteenth-century mercantile
salt fish operation that the Queen herself had opened the day
before. The rain was beginning to fall again, and as I drove into
Petty Harbour proper, past the street hockey goals hand-made
from discarded gillnets and dried-up porch planks, past the houses
that almost touched the road, I couldn't take my eyes off the ocean.
I had work to do, people to call. Cabot Martin had given me the
names of several fishermen in town who'd be happy to talk about
the death of the cod, and I had every intention of looking them up.
But I was sick—I was making my way through a bottle of Maalox
a day—and I was tired. I was done talking, done asking questions.
I wanted to go home.

I sat in my car, the wipers beating time, watching a lone fish
boat bob its way along the aptly named Motion Bay, just beyond
Petty Harbour. When the winds and the currents were right, the
bay and harbour could get a mean swell going. I took out a piece
of paper, and just for the hell of it, made a list of who was to blame
for the death of Canada's fisheries:

1. Commercial fishermen
2. Native fishermen
3. Sport fishermen
4. Commercial sport fishermen
5. The federal government
6. Less so, the provincial governments
7. Unnamed but incompetent bureaucrats at the Department of
   Fisheries and Oceans

8. Unnamed but incompetent scientists
9. The wealthy merchant class, exploiting the fishermen-workers
10. Hungry seals
11. Hungry consumers with their unsatiable lust for fish sticks
12. The Japanese, with their unsatiable lust for sushi
13. Capitalist factory owners, polluting our oceans
14. Poachers
15. Foreign fishermen, fishing within Canada's three-, twelve- or two-hundred-mile limits
16. Foreign fishermen fishing outside of Canada's three-, twelve- or two-hundred-mile limits
17. El Niño or other evil ocean currents
18. The greenhouse effect resulting from holes in the ozone— caused by car, truck and motorcycle owners; airline companies and their passengers; chemical propellant deodorant users; and capitalist factory owners
19. Loggers
20. Smokers
21. Loggers who smoke
22. Farmers
23. Farmers who smoke with loggers
24. People with no ownership stake in the resource
25. People with an ownership stake in the resource
26. Americans in general; or to be more specific, "rich" Americans, or to be really specific, an orthodontist from Omaha named Murray

With so many people out to destroy the resource, and only a handful of crusading writers and television personalities to protect it, no wonder our fish are in trouble.

My drive to Petty Harbour was the culmination of two days where nothing went right. It was the day after the *Matthew*'s arrival. That ceremony had run a little long, causing me to miss several important interviews in St. John's. So I headed to the library to do some research, but it was closed. I figured the writing was on the wall; I called the Air Canada office to change my ticket to an earlier flight. They were booked solid.

I'd spent the night awake in my hotel room, my stomach had swollen up to the size of a small buoy, the combined effects of jet lag and too much coffee, I supposed. I'd waddled down to George Street to find some way to kill time, and tried to get into a blues club called Fat Cats. But it was sold out, so I settled on a karaoke bar and disco named Sundance. It was a nightclub—not my kind of place—packed with sweating Newfies, high on screech and shooters, crooning to tunes like "He Ain't Heavy, He's My Brother," "Paradise by the Dashboard Lights" and the obligatory "New York, New York," and dancing up a storm: you haven't lived until you've seen a room full of St. John's finest citizens, dancing in unison and singing along in a drunken brogue to "Hey, Macarena," then effortlessly switching to a flawless jig as the DJ— who by now had lost his perfect AM radio voice—cued another song, and sang along, off key, into the mike:

> I's the b'y that builds the boat,
> And I's the b'y that sails her!
> I's the b'y that catches the fish
> And takes 'em home to Liza.

Hip your partner Sally Tibbo!
Hip your partner Sally Brown!
Fogo, Twillingate, Morton's Harbour,
All around the circle!

I was about to leave, when out of the blue a huge bearded man grabbed me by the arm. Now, experience has taught me that when an enormous man grabs you roughly in a bar, he's not about to make your day any brighter, so I twisted quickly, breaking free of the grip, and bolted for the door. I tried to push my way out through the stream of leather-coated partyers, but just as I was about to dive into the glaring light of the street, I felt his hand on my arm again.

"Chris," he called. "It's me, Art."

I looked at the man, trying to place his face. "Art?" I repeated, and suddenly it hit me. He was fifteen years older and forty pounds heavier, but it was Art Borders all right, who'd worked with me umpteen years ago on Uncle Roger's boat.

"Good god," I said. "It's a funny world."

"Everybody says that," he said, slapping my shoulder with his huge mitt. "But nobody laughs."

I don't want your maggoty fish,
That's no good for winter;
I could buy as good as that
Down in Bonavista . . .

Art invited me back to his table and bought me a couple of beers. He had changed a lot over the years. I remembered a skinny teenager, although admittedly, he had a maturity beyond his years. Now, while he wasn't a real Newfie, he fitted the image perfectly, almost too well, like an actor hired to play the part for a Hollywood movie. He was broad and squat, with a thick, thick beard, a face scraped red from the wind, and green-brown eyes that flowed as deep as the ocean. He was the kind of guy you'd want piloting your boat through a storm-swept sea, the kind of guy you'd want on your side if a brawl broke out on the floor of the Sundance discotheque. Art had moved to Newfoundland ten years earlier, he said, after marrying a girl from Corner Brook. The marriage didn't set well, but after the divorce, Art had decided to stay on The Rock. He'd bought a boat, picking it up for a song from a guy who just wanted out, and had set himself up in the fishing business. He'd ridden the cod out for as long as he could, but even under the moratorium he said that things were going well. Like a lot of guys, he'd switched to scallops and snow crabs after the government closed the cod fishery down, and now he was making more than he ever made off the cod. I asked him if he was taken off guard by the closures.

"It wasn't no surprise," he said, pausing to take a long draw from his pint of Iron Horse. "The fishermen could see it coming. You were going out there catching nothing or next to nothing, and what you did catch was mostly small or sick. No. You didn't need no scientist to tell you that there was something wrong. Still, I hated to see them close it. I'm just as lazy as the next guy, and the thought of having to figure out a new way to make a living gave me the creeps."

I asked him about the limited openings that were going on, conveniently scheduled just before a federal election. What did the fishermen think of that?

"Some folks say that the opening was just politics, a pre-election ploy, and of course it was. Every decision ever made by the government is a *political* decision, so what's the big surprise. But I'll tell you, I was talking to some fishermen down Placentia Bay way, and they said the cod fishing was pretty good. Then of course, fishermen are all liars, so who the hell knows."

Art grew silent and took a couple of long swigs of his beer. "You know, I want you to write something down for the people who read your book. I want you to tell them that this is a job for me. I get so tired of people treating me like some kind of political statement or cultural relic. We're just trying to make a living; we're no meaner or less concerned about the environment or heroic or wiser or more ambitious than anyone else."

I didn't get back to my hotel until near on three in the morning, and I had a hard time getting to sleep—my stomach seemed like it was going to explode. Art had offered to take me out on his boat the next day, and said that if I promised to keep my mouth shut, he'd take me to a place where we could catch some cod. I weighed my options. I knew that it wouldn't be strictly legal to catch a cod. But on the other hand, I felt that it was important to the Royal Fishin' Commission that I at least go along as an observer. On top of that moral dilemma, I was supposed to interview the Queen and Prince Philip aboard the royal yacht *Britannia* at 11:00 a.m. sharp. The Prince was an avid angler, his press secretary told me, and was particularly interested in hearing about my Royal Fishin' Commission. It was a tremendous opportunity, but—screw the Prince. What had he ever done for me? I'd told Art to sign me up; he had himself a deckhand for a day.

The North Atlantic cod is the fishery that got away. Everybody wants to know what went wrong. The real question is, what went right?

The years following Confederation had been tough for Newfoundland. The salt cod industry continued to decline, and with it went the inshore fishery that sustained the economic life of the outports. While both the federal and provincial governments stressed the importance of the inshore fisheries, private enterprise pursued another, more profitable course of action. Over time, two main fisheries had developed in Newfoundland: the inshore one, which was based in the outports and relied on dories and other small boats using small lines and cod traps; and the offshore fishery, which relied on fleets of schooners using mostly longlines. The private operators realized that to be competitive in a world more interested in fish sticks and fillets than salt cod, they'd have to concentrate on the high-volume offshore fishery.

By Confederation, Newfoundland wasn't the only fishing fleet in the sea. The world's fishery was growing more and more sophisticated, to the point that much of the processing could be done at sea. By 1960, Newfoundland offshore fishermen were competing shoulder to shoulder with boats from other parts of Canada, Russia, the United States, Britain, Spain, France, Portugal, Poland, Italy, Germany, Denmark, Japan and Iceland—fourteen hundred in all in 1962. This put tremendous pressure on the resource; during the first forty years of the century, the total world catch of northern cod stocks hovered around half a million tons per year. By 1955, that number had more than doubled, and by the end of the decade the annual catch was approaching the two-million-ton mark and more than two thousand boats were choking the waters off Newfoundland. It used to be that New-foundland sent its cod to feed the world; now the world came to Newfoundland and the cod, quite frankly, were getting fed up.

As early as 1949, the Canadian government was concerned over the pressure on the east coast cod stocks, and with the support of the United States, Ottawa convinced a dozen fishing nations— Newfoundland included—to endorse the International Convention for the Northwest Atlantic Fisheries. Signing countries pledged to conserve the stocks in order to maintain "a maximum sustained yield," a bureaucratic oxymoron on the level of "friendly fire" and "CBC special." The countries that signed the convention got together again and formed the International Commission for the Northwest Atlantic Fisheries, to monitor the ongoing health of the cod stocks.

Ottawa was making its presence felt at home by cultivating the complex web of subsidies and assistance programs for the industry, which by the 1950s, when combined with various levels of provincial support, was equivalent to about 80 percent of the value of the landed fish. That ratio continued to rise through the 1960s, to the point that by the end of the decade some critics claimed the value of subsidies actually exceeded the landed value of the cod.

In 1967, the federal government did a complete about-face. In the final report of the Royal Commission on the Economic State and Prospects of Newfoundland and Labrador, it withdrew its support for the inshore fishery and recommended that the people of the outports be resettled in larger communities catering to offshore fishing and processing. The bottom line, the report stated, was that the fishery was "the chief economic liability of the province."

The cod fishery peaked in 1968, when the world catch was upward of three million tons. After that, the fishery began its steady decline. In order to maintain past volumes, fishermen chased an ever-increasing array of fish: herring, mackerel, capelin, haddock, redfish. The fish stick men didn't care, as long as they had the volume they needed. These fish, though, were worth less than cod, so the lot of the average fisherman declined.

Nothing seemed to slow the decline, so in 1971, Canada moved to protect the two biggest trouble spots by declaring the Gulf of St. Lawrence and the Bay of Fundy Canadian-only fishing zones. By the mid-1970s, the entire groundfish fishery was in turmoil, and rigid quotas were the order of the day, while governments still talked of maximum sustainable yield. In 1974, the cod catches hit record lows; the fishery had hit rock bottom. In an effort to take charge of the situation, Canada and three other North Atlantic coastal countries—Denmark, France and the United States—declared two-hundred-mile fishing zones. But the scope of these zones wasn't cut and dried. Because of the St. Pierre and Miquelon Islands, France and Canada shared a huge chunk of the restricted area, which neither wanted to give up. Meanwhile, other fishing nations weren't about to walk away from the North Atlantic without a fight, and over time, Ottawa has had to concede quotas within the limit to buy the compliance of the rest of the fishing world. Nevertheless, as recently as 1991, ships from Spain, Portugal and Russia, fishing just outside the two-hundred-mile limit, took one-quarter of the total northern cod catch, breaking every known treaty.

It seemed like the situation in the cod fishery couldn't get any worse.

Then, disaster struck.

Sods and rinds to cover your flake,
Cake and tea for supper,
Codfish in the spring o' the year
Fried in maggoty butter . . .

The Newfoundland processors have done their homework. They've read the research that shows how readily western consumers will switch from one species of fish to another, particularly when it comes minced, breaded, deep-fried, frozen and stuffed in an attractive box. While the dense schools of cod are the perfect victims for the processors, the industry has chased after a parade of nubile young fish—capelin, haddock, pollock, herring, halibut, turbot—to help it maintain its massive manufacturing quotas. By the late 1960s, as the problems in the cod fishery became evident to practically everybody outside of the government, Newfoundland's groundfish catch approached the catch volumes for cod, and by 1970, the annual groundfish catch began to exceed that of cod on a regular basis.

Capelin are members of the smelt family, and are an essential part of the cod fishery. These small fish, which rarely grow to more than nine inches in length, are the main food source for the cod. In the summer, they move from deep waters to the gravel beaches of Newfoundland to spawn, with the hungry cod hot on their fins, and thus have supported the inshore fishery for centuries. Capelin look similar to other smelt; they have narrow bodies, finely tapered heads, and big eyes almost a third the breadth of their heads. But pressure from the offshore fishery, which uses them extensively for longliner bait, and other forms of overfishing have led to a decline in their numbers.

Haddock look like designer versions of their cousins, the Atlantic cod. They have sharper, more flamboyant fins, a slightly longer face, with bigger, more beautiful eyes, and a rakish well-trimmed barb that lends the fish a bohemian air. Haddock are easy to distinguish from other groundfish by the sporty black pinstripe that runs the length of their body. The average commercially caught haddock runs a foot or two in length, and weighs up to five pounds. While even ten-pound haddock are unusual, the odd one will reach weights of almost forty pounds. The haddock has always been an important part of the North Atlantic fishery, probably second only to the cod; in 1962, at the height of the fish frenzy, fishermen took 305 million pounds of haddock out of east coast waters. By the 1970s, haddock stocks were suffering, and in 1970, they were one of the first of the groundfish to become subject to quotas set by the International Commission for the North Atlantic Fisheries. Extensive overfishing by deepwater vessels on both sides of the two-hundred-mile limit has led to a decline in the number of haddock.

Pollock is a distant cousin to the cod, and looks kind of like a haddock on a good hair day. The feature that stands out the most on these fish is a white stripe running from gill to tail. Pollock, which are often marketed to consumers as Boston bluefish, are slightly larger than cod and haddock, growing to an average length of three and a half feet, with a weight of around ten pounds. They are also one of the more popular groundfish, becoming increasingly popular as cod stocks disappeared; extensive overfishing by deep-water vessels on both sides of the two-hundred-mile limit has led to a decline in pollock stocks.

The turbot, also known as the Greenland halibut, is a flatfish that can reach three and a half feet in length and weigh up to twenty-five pounds. It looks similar to the halibut, and shares this fish's concave tail, a feature unique among the flatfish in Newfound-land's waters. It's a deepwater fish that prefers the cold, cold waters of the Arctic and North Atlantic. While it has been fished commercially in Newfoundland for decades—by 1950, the turbot catch already equalled one million pounds—it came to prominence in 1995 when this ugly little fish found itself the target of affec-tions from two rival suitors. In defiance of quotas set by the inter-national commission, Spanish trawlers were fishing for turbot just within Canada's two-hundred-mile limit. Armed fisheries officials boarded one trawler, the *Estia*, arrested the crew, and seized the ship. It was a public relations triumph for then Fisheries Minister and current Newfoundland premier Brian Tobin, proof positive that he wasn't going to take no shit from nobody, not even a Spanish trawler captain, when it came to such a vital resource as Newfoundland's turbot. British Columbia's turbot was a different matter. Terry Glavin reports in *Dead Reckoning: Confronting the Crisis in Pacific Fisheries* that at the same time Brian Tobin was putting on his show of strength for the cameras, British Columbia fishermen were routinely, and legally, dumping thousands of pounds of dead Pacific turbot into the ocean. The turbot, better known in British Columbia as arrowtooth flounder, was the victim of by-catch—unwanted fish caught by fishermen in the pursuit of something else. Glavin writes that while the contradictory treatment of the two turbot species seems hypocritical, it made "perfect business sense":

> In the North Atlantic, the Spanish were protesting a quota system that favoured Canadian ships, and Canada wanted to drive the Spaniards off the Grand Banks in order to secure raw supplies for its own badly weakened East Coast processing industry. In the North Pacific, dumping turbot can mean the difference between returning to port with a valuable fish in the hold, or coming back with a hold full of highly perishable fish that fetch as little as nine cents a pound.

Extensive overfishing by deepwater vessels on both sides of the two-hundred-mile limit has led to a decline in turbot stocks.

✓

Susan White, she's out of sight
Her petticoat wants a border;
Old Sam Oliver, in the dark
He kissed her in the corner . . .

✓

Something went terribly wrong. Somehow, the figures didn't add up. In 1977, the Atlantic fisheries commission had set a target to rebuild what it called the "spawning biomass" of the north Atlantic cod. The commission believed that restrictive quotas would allow the cod stocks to rejuvenate, and set as its target 1.65 million tons of mature cod, seven years and older. In 1987, the DFO estimated that the strategy was working, and this "biomass" had already reached more than 830,000 tons. But in 1992, the DFO dropped a bombshell. They cited an "overestimation of stock abundance" dating back as early as the late 1970s, and now believed that the total amount of mature cod equalled about twenty-four thousand tons. A little while later Ottawa announced a two-year moratorium on the cod fisheries. Five years later that moratorium is still in effect. There've been a few breaks; for a couple of days in the fall of 1997, the DFO opened the cod up for food fishing only. And a month before I arrived in Newfoundland, the federal Liberal party, in a shallow attempt to buy votes on the east coast, allowed a partial reopening of the south coast fishery.

While these openings might just be blips on the ecological radar screen, there are some signs that the cod are starting to recover. Although there's no hard scientific evidence to date, fishermen told me that they've noticed cod in places where there hasn't been any for years. That's what they say, anyways.

But of course, as we all know, fishermen are liars.

Art called to cancel our fish trip. He'd won $430,000 in the lottery, he said. He'd already sold his boat and bought his airline ticket. He was going to Hollywood, he said; he was going to follow his life-long dream.

"But what about the fish?" I asked.

"Screw the fish. I'm gonna go write sitcoms."

I'd hoped to end on a positive note. I'd hoped to discover something in the swells off Petty Harbour that would give me cause to feel optimistic about the future of this country and its fish.

But from where I sat, I couldn't see anything worthwhile.

I wanted a better view, so I got out of my car and edged my way down the face of a steep bluff. I came to a small crevice in the rock where a clutch of North Atlantic puffins were seeking shelter from the wind. "It's okay, little birdy," I said in a soothing voice. "I won't hurt you." But the birds had heard that song and dance before, and flew off. I watched the waves hit the shore for a few moments, not certain of what I was looking for, just knowing that I wanted to end it all on a positive note, find something powerful or optimistic or profound to say, something touching or pleasantly ironic. Out of the corner of my eye, I thought I saw something shimmer for a moment. A cod maybe, down there in the kelp bed, or—who knows—a salmon or perch or whitefish or brook trout or muskie. I stared intently at the spot, waiting patiently, quietly, so as to not scare the fish, waiting, watching. But there was nothing. A figment of my imagination. Another moment had passed by, leaving me with nothing except one more story about the one that got away. I heard the low roar of a jet engine, and a moment later a plane hove into sight, low over the village, on its final approach for the St. John's airport. Next stop Victoria; all aboard. I turned to go, but was suddenly struck with the strangest urge. I don't know what hit me, but I began to sing, first softly, then as my confidence grew, louder and louder until I was serenading the wild sea with a thundering storm of song:

Oh, I's the b'y that builds the boat,
And I's the b'y that sails her!
I's the b'y that catches the fish
And takes 'em home to Liza . . .

And as I was singing, the most remarkable thing happened. Across the bay, I heard a lone voice join me. Then another, from a different direction, and another, and another . . .

Hip your partner Sally Tibbo!
Hip your partner Sally Brown!
Fogo, Twillingate, Morton's Harbour,
All around the circle . . .

Soon, the men, women and children of Petty Harbour, and parts of Motion Bay, were joined in song. We continued on into the night, single, separate voices, distant but united, continued on through the howls of the sleep-deprived dogs, on past the complaints of unneighbourly neighbours, who first loudly implored us to "shut-the-fuck-up" and quickly escalated from there, until the RCMP showed up with two howling dogs of their own and asked us to please stop singing—and still we continued on and on until they picked me up and carried me to the cruiser, and carefully placed me in the back, making sure I didn't bump my head on the way in, and as we drove off down the highway I kept singing all the way, and I could hear the good men and women and children of Petty Harbour too, until their voices faded in the distance, and all that I could hear was the sound of my own voice, and the police dogs a-howling, and the deep, rich baritone of the one cop who just couldn't resist a song. And so the Royal Fishin' Commission closed, with a police honour guard escorting me not to jail—for even in Canada they don't arrest a man for singing late at night—but to the airport. The police had talked to the airlines, who'd made a special exception, and found me a seat on the very next flight. Finally, my wish was coming. I was leaving the fish—and my Royal Fishin' Commission—behind. My work was finished. I was going home.

Chapter 11

Carpe Carpum

I would like to have dinner with the man
who didn't follow Christ, the one who,
When Jesus said: Follow me and I
will make you fishers of men, decided
to go fishing instead . . .

—"Dinner," by Patrick Lane

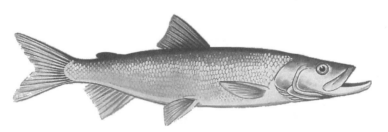

Inconnu

Final recommendations of the
Royal Fishin' Commission

S itting in my office in Victoria, British Columbia, and the news is not good. It's the day after Remembrance Day, 1997—the thirteenth anniversary of my own father's death by heart attack at age fifty-eight—and the headline in the *Times-Colonist* reads: "Salmon numbers are sinking." The story tells of the low returns of spawning coho and chinook runs in Goldstream River, five miles north of my house. I'd noticed the problem myself the day before, when Barb, me and the boys went for a hike along the riverside. Usually the creek is choked with salmon pushing their way upstream, while the shore is littered with fish corpses. But on this day there weren't any fish on the shore, and there couldn't have been any more than a few hundred in the water. "Where are the salmons?" Charlie and Tavish ask. "Gloop gla," the baby, Keating, pipes in. But I have no answers.

And so, forgive me if I'm feeling a little gloomy as I prepare this final report of the Royal Fishin' Commission. But I guess I'm losing my patience. In the entire history of the world there has never been a good fish stock that hasn't been overfished or otherwise destroyed. If in the next few years we find fish on Mars, you can bet we'll have fished the planet dry by the year 2099. The Royal Fishin' Commission is therefore reluctant to make any recommendations. But here goes.

1. Canadians should invent a new kind of fast food, one that has nothing to do with fish. In fact, to benefit the whole world, it should have nothing to do with animal protein whatsoever. Ideally, it would be made from sewage, discarded rubber tires, or carpet remnants—and taste a lot like chicken.

2. Failing that, let's get our priorities straight. Let's give those people who most need the fish the greatest access to them. That means that, just like in Saskatchewan, the native and other subsistence fisheries should have priority over commercial and sport interests.

3. Meanwhile, the government should set up a Board of Nomenclature to give all the fish in the country really uninteresting sounding or disgusting names. For example, a food fish like the Atlantic cod might become "spleenfish," "leperbreath" or the "yellow-crusted barf," while a sportfish like the chinook salmon might be known as "mellowfish" or "dead weight."

4. Just a silly idea, but let's charge anglers way more money for their licences, so they're actually paying an equitable rate for the amount of public time and money that goes to monitoring and maintaining the sportfisheries. The money we make can be rolled back into conservation and habitat restoration programs.

5. Let's get rid of the current fisheries bureaucracies, particularly the Fisheries Minister. What do we need one of those for? The industry has no impact on the national economy. It would make a lot more sense to have a Minister of Fast Food. Instead, let's make the DFO a small branch of the Ministry of Tourism or, better yet, the Ministry of Employment and Immigration, since in most parts of the country, commercial fishing is a make-work project anyway.

6. Let's extend our two-hundred-mile limit to include the entire world. That way, all the fish would be ours.

7. Catch-and-release for everyone, including commercial fishermen.

8. Let's just kill all the fish right now. Then we can feel bad for
the fish, sorry for ourselves and get on with our lives.

9. Let's set up a proper Royal Commission to look at Canada's
fisheries. This time, we'll spare no expense. Of course, we'll
need to hire someone to run the thing, someone with extensive experience doing this sort of thing; I'll gladly forward a
short list to the prime minister. And when I say short, I mean
short.

The preceding recommendations respectfully submitted by:

Chris Gudgeon
Chair, Canadian Royal Fishin' Commission

Dear Chris:

Having a great time in Florida.

The Americans are really wonderful people once you get to know them. The fish farm is really taking off. I think it's the wave of the future.

Lamont's divorce finally came through, and we're already planning our wedding. Hope you can come.

Good luck with your new book!

Love and Fishes,
Lil and Lamont

P.S. Who says that the French and English can't live together in harmony?